IS FAITH OBSOLETE?

Books by Robert McAfee Brown
Published by The Westminster Press

Is Faith Obsolete?
Religion and Violence
The Pseudonyms of God
The Collect'd Writings of St. Hereticus
The Significance of the Church
  (Layman's Theological Library)
The Bible Speaks to You
P. T. Forsyth: Prophet for Today

IS FAITH OBSOLETE?

ROBERT McAFEE BROWN

THE WESTMINSTER PRESS
PHILADELPHIA

Scripture quotations from the Revised Standard Version of the Bible are copyright, 1946 and 1952, by the Division of Christian Education of the National Council of Churches and are used by permission.

Published by the Westminster Press ®
Philadelphia, Pennsylvania

Printed in the United States of America

Library of Congress Cataloging in Publication Data

Brown, Robert McAfee, 1920–
    Is faith obsolete?

    Includes bibliographical references.
    1. Faith. I. Title.
BV4637.B8   234′.2   74–13420
ISBN 0–664–20715–4

To choose what is difficult all one's days
As if it were easy, that is faith. . . .

—*W. H. Auden*

CONTENTS

ACKNOWLEDGMENTS

      Part of the material that follows was first presented as the Frank H. Caldwell Lectures at Louisville Presbyterian Theological Seminary in April 1971, a lectureship in which I feel particularly honored to have participated since I had previously worked with Dr. Caldwell in some interdenominational activities. Professor Arnold Rhodes was most helpful in planning for the lectureship, and he and President Albert Winn, together with their wives, made my stay on the seminary campus a cordial one. I must also express thanks to a number of students who took exception to almost everything I said, thereby forcing me to do considerable rethinking before the material appeared in print—a gratitude I feel more cordially in retrospect than I probably did at the time, but a gratitude that I hope translates into a more comprehensible text.

The material has undergone major revision and expansion in its transformation from the oral to the printed word, and most of what is in Chapters Four and Five, as well as the Epilogue, is new. Documentation and bibliographical suggestions will be found in the notes and comments. I have already noted the benefactions made possible by my seminarian critics; in addition, portions of the material have been helped by the response of a student-pastor seminar at Carroll College, Waukesha, Wisconsin, laypersons at the First Presbyterian Church of Durham, North Carolina, and students and faculty at the University of Alabama, Tuscaloosa, Alabama. I am most grateful of all to my friend and colleague, Professor Jerry A. Irish, of the Department of Religious Studies at Stanford University, for a critical reading of the entire manuscript. I am indebted to Linda Williams and Karen Friedland for bringing order out of the chaos I gave them to type. I must also express deep appreciation to the Office of the Dean of Humanities and Sciences at Stanford University for a grant in the summer of 1973, which freed me to do major revisions; and to my wife, for taking a job during the following fall, when I was on half salary trying to pull the whole thing together.

Portions of the material, in somewhat different form, have appeared in the following journals: *Internationale Dialog Zeitschrift, Concurrence, Theology Today, Religion in Life, A.D., The Christian Century.*

The reader should not be fooled. This is a "Christian" book in the sense that although it discusses faith in a variety of situations and from a variety of standpoints, my own faith is Christian and (particularly in Chapters Four and Five) I am primarily engaged with problems of Christian faith. I have made a special effort, however, to deal with the subject matter in such a way that non-Christians (whether Marxists, humanists, Jews, or whatever) can read and, I hope, appropriate much of what is said. Therefore, as much as considerations of space allow, I have provided examples of my themes from faith-traditions other than my own.

In particular, the early part of the book illustrates my own increasing engagement with the Jewish tradition. The early church made a decision (symbolized in the controversy over circumcision) that the Gentile need not first become a Jew in order to become a Christian. I am no longer sure that was a wise decision. I think we must immerse ourselves ever more fully in what Judaism is, if we are to understand what Christianity might become. So I make no apology to Christians for many Jewish references. I apologize only to Jews if I have misunderstood, or have appeared to touch with profane hands, what can only be apprehended with reverence, awe, and wonder.

ROBERT MCAFEE BROWN

Stanford, California

INTRODUCTION

The Decline and Fall of Faith; or, Clearing Away the Underbrush

(faith and theology)

> And now abideth faith, hope, love, these three;
> but the most neglected of these is faith.
> —*St. Paul, revised*

It may seem foolish to introduce the formidable word "theology" even in the parenthetical subheading of an introduction, particularly if one is inclined to wonder, as I frequently do, whether sin came into the world, not because Eve offered Adam the forbidden fruit, but because she chose to engage the serpent in a theological discussion.

I run the risk, however, because I believe it important to "position" the present discussion within the ever so rapidly changing theological scene. Those who have no interest in such niceties can, without serious loss, skip immediately to Chapter One; those with an interest in things theological are invited to linger briefly over these opening pages.

FAITH IN DECLINE

In a perceptive and somewhat wistful essay published a number of years ago entitled "Thursday's Child," William Hamilton noted that America is often described as a place "without a sense of having a past and without a sense of being able to count on a stable future." Building on that insight, he went on to comment:

> Hope is the way of declaring one's future to be open and assured, and love is the way of standing before your neighbor in the present moment. Taking faith, hope and love together, the feeling is that the American theologian can really live in only one of them at a time, perhaps only one in a lifetime. If this is so, and if it is also so that as an American he is fated to be a man without a sense of past or future, then it follows that the theologian today and tomorrow is a man without faith, without hope, with only the present, with only love to guide him.
>   I propose that we should not only acknowledge but will this faithlessness. . . .

There are a number of things in this statement with which it is possible to take issue, but we can accept the descriptive truth of Hamilton's statement that faith, as some kind of reliance on the *past* (which is his implied definition), is increasingly questioned in our time. If we adopt a further rough equation of hope as a posture for viewing the *future*, and love as a means of dealing with the *present*, we are left, according to William Hamilton, with nothing but love. A strong case is made for love, by Hamilton and others, and a stronger case can be made for hope than he acknowledges. But who in this day and age feels constrained to make a strong case for faith? Faith is, at best, in eclipse, and may truly be in the midst of decline and fall. Let us look briefly at how this has come to be.

In a period not long past that already seems like ancient history, the period of so-called "neo-orthodoxy," there can be little doubt that faith was preeminent, not only in St. Paul's sequence but in the regnant theologies of the time. Barth, Brunner, Bultmann, Bonhoeffer, the Niebuhrs, Tillich, and others, whatever things separated them, all insisted that there is a historical past to which we not only can but must relate ourselves, that Christianity involves "faith seeking understanding," and that the Biblical heritage, transmitted through the church, provides the locus for appropriating the faith thus discovered. Such faith was uniformly dissociated from "assent to propositions" (whether of the Catholic scholastic or Protestant fundamentalist variety), and it had a lively quality of trust and commitment ("truth as encounter" was a favorite phrase). At the same time, faith had a clearly discernible content which it was the business of theologians to describe and transmit. The object of this faith, the one to whom commitment was pledged, was (even though a living, present reality) one who had acted in a decisive way in the *past*. There was a "once-for-allness" about his action that made necessary no new revelation in the future and required only a continual outworking of the implications of the past event for use in the present.

HOPE ON THE RISE

At almost the precise moment that Hamilton was announcing not only that such a faith had become impossible for American theologians but also that hope must be jettisoned as well, a movement was coming to birth in Germany called "the theology of hope." It was nourished particularly by the writings of the Protestant theologian Jürgen Moltmann and, to a somewhat lesser extent, the Roman Catholic theologian Johannes Metz. Moltmann in particular drew not only upon Biblical resources but also upon the writings of a Marxist philosopher, Ernst Bloch, whose huge work, *Das Prinzip Hoffnung* ("The Hope Principle"), had been attracting widespread attention since its publication a few years earlier. Due in large part to the theological following that Moltmann has attracted, it is safe to say that the theological pendulum has shifted strongly from faith to hope, which is another way of saying that attention has moved from past to future.

It is to Moltmann's credit that he has refused to let his concern for the future blind him to the importance of learning lessons from the past, and his major work, *Theology of Hope,* is essentially a book of Biblical theology, drawing heavily on Israel's past and on the centrality for hope of Jesus' resurrection. Thus in Moltmann's own theology a creative tension between past and future has been maintained.

But one of the problems of theological movements is that the virtues of the fathers are not always appropriated by their theological offspring, and the danger in the present enthusiasm for a theology of hope is that the tension between past and future will be lessened, and that the emerging theology will be so oriented to the future as to lose sight of lessons and warnings that come out of the past. Just as the emphasis on faith tended—among second-generation neo-orthodox—to be overly pessimistic and even exclusivistic, so the emphasis on hope may become overly optimistic and even directionless, sacrificing the rootage that comes out of the signs, signals, and experiences that preceded it.

LOVE IN JEOPARDY

There has been a strong challenge to the relevance of faith from the past, and we have just issued warnings about the adequacy of hope for the future. It might seem, therefore, that we are left with nothing but love in the present. This, as we have seen, is the line that was taken a few years ago by proponents of the short-lived "death of God" theology, of which Hamilton was one of the most sensitive interpreters, but it is more persuasively argued today by others for whom faith in the past is intellectually impossible no matter how reassuring it might be, and hope for the future is unrealistic, no matter how desirable it might be. They argue that we are left with nothing but love.

We may note in passing that there is something startling about asserting that "we are left with nothing but love," since it could be argued that if we really had love, little else would be needed. Even Augustine could summarize the content of Christian living with the injunction, "Love, and do as you please," and many people, however wrong they may think Paul was about other things, would agree that he was at least right to assert, in evaluating faith, hope, and love, that "the greatest of these is love."

But if "we are left with nothing but love," it soon becomes clear that we have not solved but only stated a profound dilemma of our times, which is that love has exceedingly rough going when it tries to hold its own in a world dominated by power. On the face of it, it is hard to see why love should be declared normative when it is so easily scarred and even destroyed in the rough-and-tumble world. "Make Love, Not War" may be an appealing slogan, but it can be effective only if someone else sees to it that warriors are kept under control. When enough people agree that power comes from the barrel of a gun, love is likely to be at the mercy of those carrying the guns. Confusion is further compounded when we note the bewilderment with which the advocates of love alone try to distinguish between love, sex, lust, caring, and sharing. Many of the oppressed in today's world describe love scornfully as a middle-class copout, possible only for those in comfortable circumstances who are insulated (probably by police power) from the likelihood that anything will threaten their comfort.

Is Faith Obsolete?

This cursory inspection of the recent past suggests, then, that while hope seems dominant on the theological scene and love on the ethical scene, the adequacy of both can be called into question, and it suggests further that faith even more than hope or love is under attack. Faith, to many, has become obsolete, and an "appeal to faith" is likely to be interpreted as either failing to do justice to patent empirical realities or prescribing a wistful and impossible return to outworn convictions.

We can summarize the suspicion that faith is obsolete by asking two kinds of questions:

On the one hand we may ask, after genuine struggle: "How can I possibly have faith in God?" Behind the question are all the ongoing formidable obstacles to belief, heightened in their intensity by the times in which we live: the ugly reality of evil, the lack of solid empirical evidence, the archaic nature of the world view that much faith implies, and so on. In such a situation, *faith is held to be important but not possible.*

On the other hand we may ask, after equally genuine struggle: "Even if I could have faith in God, what difference would it make?" Behind this question is the conviction, not that faith is difficult, but simply that faith is irrelevant. The notion that if we do not believe in God we must end up in despair is countered by the lives of many happy pagans; the notion that faith empowers us to good conduct is countered by the lives of many evil Christians. In such a situation, *faith is held to be possible but not important.*

In the one case, faith is too dear; in the other, too cheap. In both cases it is remote. And their names are legion who claim to get along quite well without it.

FAITH, HOPE, LOVE—
IN SOMETHING LIKE THAT ORDER

It may be that part of the reason for the decline and fall of faith is due to misunderstanding. Even in our brief discussion thus far we have used the word "faith" in a sufficient variety of ways to multiply such misunderstanding—a fault we will try to correct in Chapter One. We can, and we should, disavow certain misunderstandings of faith, such as the schoolboy definition of faith as "believing what you know ain't true," or the definition offered by Dorothy Sayers in her modern catechism:

> Q: What is faith?
> A: Resolutely shutting your eyes to scientific fact.
> Q: What is the human intellect?
> A: A barrier to faith.

But there is clearly more at stake than the repudiation of inadequate definitions, and the burden of the pages that follow is that, however profound our reasons for disavowing it, we do need a recovery of the reality of faith, and that, far from being obsolete, it is the thing most needful for our times. The argument to be advanced need not be summarized here, and it will stand or fall in its own unfolding, but since (except on a few occasions) faith will be considered by itself, in apparent isolation from hope and love, it is important to conclude our introduction with a brief consideration of their interrelationship.

It was surely a sound instinct that led the apostle Paul, even in a "hymn to love," to begin his concluding summary sequence with a reference to faith, for, whatever else we determine faith to be, we must surely understand it as a way of appropriating something that is already available to us, provided for us out of the past, and about which we make some kind of decision, for or against. It is out of whatever *faith* we affirm that we can look ahead to what is still to come and (depending on the content of the faith) be enabled to adopt a stance of *hope* for the future. And it is out of a creative tension between past and future (i.e., between faith and hope) that we can form the ingredients for deal-

ing with the present, a stance that (once again depending
on the content of the faith and hope) can be an embodiment of *love*.

It is, of course, possible to arrange the sequence in other
ways, and no one, least of all an author, is ever entitled to
put a systematic straitjacket around qualities as dynamic as
faith, hope, and love. All that really needs to be insisted
upon, for the discussion to proceed, is that faith has a ca-
pacity to undergird hope and love and to provide both the
content and the context in which they flourish most creatively. In such a situation, faith in its turn becomes a bene-
ficiary, for fruits of hope and love can nourish and deepen
the faith from which they spring, and there is considerable
evidence in human lives that such an interplay is always in
process.

Reinhold Niebuhr gives a helpful example of such interplay, and shows how rich are the possibilities of developing,
and even expanding, the mutuality that can exist between
faith, hope, and love.

> Nothing that is worth doing can be achieved in our lifetime;
> therefore we must be saved by hope. Nothing which is true
> or beautiful or good makes complete sense in any immediate
> context of history; therefore we must be saved by faith. Noth-
> ing we do, however virtuous, can be accomplished alone; there-
> fore we are saved by love. No virtuous act is quite as virtuous
> from the standpoint of our friend or foe as it is from our
> standpoint. Therefore we must be saved by the final form of
> love which is forgiveness.

The interplay is even more complex when we consider the
relationship of faith, hope, and love in communal terms. A
full examination of this dimension would take us too far
afield. But we can at least note, in highly schematized form,
the way this might work out in the community of faith, using
the Christian community as our example. In terms of classic
self-definitions of the functions of this particular community,
we get something like the following:

	means	with the church as	of the Kingdom of God as	calling for
kērygma	proclamation	announcer	past event	faith
koinōnia	community	embodier	present reality	love
diakonia	service	enabler	future possibility	hope

To do full justice to the interrelationships, however, we would need to include a fourth function of the community, i.e., liturgy, through which in an extraordinary way all the qualities we are examining are brought together in unified and holistic fashion. Thus:

	means	with the church as	of the Kingdom of God as	calling for
leitourgia	liturgy	announcer	past event	faith
	("the people's	and	and	and
	work")	embodier	present reality	love
		and	and	and
		enabler	future possibility	hope

While this theme will be touched upon at occasional points in our subsequent argument, a full treatment of the interrelationships of faith, hope, and love must be deferred to another occasion, on the assumption that enough has now been suggested to enable us, with clearer conscience, to make faith the main burden of our investigation.

CHAPTER ONE

Definitions Old and New; or, Clarifying Some Ambiguities

(faith and ourselves)

> "Faith" is a fine invention
> When Gentlemen can *see*—
> But Microscopes are Prudent
> In an Emergency.
> —*Emily Dickinson*

Once we have smiled with Emily Dickinson, we will probably want to take issue with her. Is it not more often the case that "Gentlemen" call upon faith precisely when they *cannot* "see," and that they offer faith as something to take the place of sight? To reflect upon this matter, or simply to recall the variety of ways in which we spoke about faith in the Introduction, is to be reminded forcefully of the need for careful definition of a word we will be using constantly in our discussion.

One Word—Many Uses

Here, then, is a sampling of some of the ways we use the word "faith" in our ordinary, or not-so-ordinary, conversation.

1. *"We have not yet discovered a cure for cancer, but I have faith that someday we will."*

The scientist is telling us that he trusts his methods of laboratory experimentation, that he can build on the accumulated wisdom of his predecessors, that the future is "open" to the solution of a problem that has so far defied solution, and that he will continue to dedicate his professional expertise and his life to that end.

2. *". . . the faith which was once for all delivered to the saints."*

The writer of The Letter of Jude uses this phrase to warn his readers against false teaching, to which must be opposed true teaching, i.e., "the faith . . ." Here faith is something to be believed. It is a body of material with a content. We can learn about it, appropriate it, distinguish it from its opposite. Depending on who the "saints" or true believers are, "the faith" delivered to them might be (as in this case) contained in the New Testament gospel, but it might also be contained in the collected writings of Chairman Mao, the Eightfold Path of Enlightenment, or the rule book of the International Field Hockey Association.

3. *"Faith of our fathers, living still."*

Here, too, faith sounds like a set of beliefs, but a personal relationship to those beliefs is now being established. The hymn writer is not just talking in impersonal fashion about the faith delivered to "the saints," but in highly personal fashion about the faith delivered to *"our fathers,"* in a succession to which we belong. Furthermore it is not just something delivered once for all in the past, but something out of *our* past that is "living still." The content of the faith will still be determined by who "our fathers" are (Christians, Maoists, Buddhists, or field hockey experts), but if the faith is truly important to us, we will keep it (as the hymn writer adds) "in spite of dungeon, fire, and sword." Yet more, "we will be true to thee till death." Or, to make the point succinctly: *"Keep the faith, baby!"*

4. *"Things are really rough right now, but I have faith that they will work out for the best."*

Here faith becomes the equivalent of what we call a "world view," a context or framework within which life can be lived. The world view need not be optimistic, as it is above. The conviction could also go, "Things are really rough right now and I have no faith that they will get any better," or even, "My faith is that evil wins out in the end," a conviction stated more graphically by James Thurber's character, F. Hopkinson Smith: "The claw of the seapuss gets us in the end."

5. *"It seems as though we are traveling south, but I have faith that the compass is right and that we are really traveling north-northeast."*

Faith now includes trust and reliance on an authority, even though all the experience of the speaker suggests that the authority is wrong. The degree of trust will be indicated by whether or not the speaker alters course to conform to the compass reading rather than a personal intuition.

6. *"It looks like a forgery, but I have faith in the art dealer's assertion that it is an original."*

The extent of the trust has now been enlarged. The evidence that a compass offers has a high degree of assurance behind it; compasses do not lie, cheat, change their minds, or get fooled very often. Neither do art dealers. But this one might be an exception. There is greater risk involved in this kind of faith, for it is trust in a person.

Reverse of the above situation. The sand dunes of Kitty Hawk, North Carolina, December 17, 1903: *"You'll never get it off the ground, Orville."*

7. *"We're in trouble out here, but I have faith in those guys back in Houston."*

Trust (and risk) have now been further enlarged. The astronaut who talks this way is not only trusting someone else's judgment about a piece of art, he is entrusting his own personal destiny and even survival to others.

The same thing happens when a person (*a*) undergoes anesthesia and surgery, (*b*) sits in the back seat of a moving vehicle, (*c*) eats a meal someone else has prepared, (*d*) marries, (*e*) shares a secret.

These random examples cumulatively begin to tell us something about the meaning of faith as we ordinarily use the word, and what they tell us will be useful when we develop a working definition. Faith clearly has some sort of *content*, drawn out of our own experience or out of the common experience of the *past*, and our engagement with it involves us in varying degrees of *commitment* to that content, involving both *trust* and *risk*. Consequently we act on the basis of the degree of trust we possess: we continue the lab experiments, we endure dungeon, fire, and sword, we sail north-northeast, we buy the painting, we stay out of the airplane, we remain confident in the space capsule.

A Classic Definition of Faith

These examples, drawn from a variety of kinds of faith, are also helpful in thinking more specifically about what it might mean to have faith in God. Here again, we discover a similar invoking of a reality that has preceded us, grounded in the past as well as the present, and involving a similar interplay between content and commitment. And even though we must temporarily shift our vocabulary in order to talk about faith in God, it will be worth the effort if we can thereby discover the close similarity between many of the concerns expressed in a classic definition of faith in God and the concerns we have just been examining.

The definition we shall examine is John Calvin's (none more classic than he), and it is found in his *Institutes of the Christian Religion*, the definitive edition of which was published in 1559. Faith, Calvin says, is

> a firm and certain knowledge of God's benevolence toward us, founded upon the truth of the freely given promise in Christ, both revealed to our minds and sealed upon our hearts through the Holy Spirit.

We can find at least five things in this highly compressed definition that can help us in our quest for a fuller understanding of faith.

1. Faith is *knowledge*. It is not amorphous or blurry. It has a content. In Calvin's case, the content is defined as "God's benevolence," his graciousness and goodwill toward his children—a point worth noting in the light of the consistently bad press Calvin has gotten for four hundred years as the purveyor of a malevolent deity.

2. Faith is *assured* knowledge. It is "firm and certain." This is the point at which contemporary persons may have great difficulty with Calvin's definition. How can one talk about "firm and certain knowledge" in a time when everything that we know and believe seems to be under attack and foundering? It is important to see clearly what Calvin means by "firm and certain knowledge." He does not mean that believers have no doubts (Calvin has some wonderfully human passages on doubt), nor that all things are crystal clear to persons of faith. He means rather that *enough* is clear so that we can trust for the rest. His illustration of our situation is graphic:

> It is like a man who, shut up in a prison into which the sun's rays shine obliquely and half obscured through a rather narrow window, is indeed deprived of the full sight of the sun. Yet his

eye dwells on its steadfast brightness, and he receives its bene-fits. Thus, bound with the fetters of an earthly body, however much we are shadowed on every side with great darkness, we are nevertheless illumined as much as need be for firm assur-ance when, to show forth his mercy, the light of God sheds even a little of its radiance.

Our knowledge is sufficient, Calvin says, when the light of God sheds "even a little" of its radiance.

3. Faith is *existential* knowledge. The word, of course, is not Calvin's, but what the word means to us today is what Calvin meant when he said that faith's knowledge was of "God's benevolence *toward us.*" Existential truth, Kierke-gaard said, is truth that is true *for me,* and Calvin's concern, at least in this regard, is similar to Kierkegaard's. Calvin dis-plays extraordinarily little interest in God as he is in himself; the concern is always with God as he is in relation to us. Before embarking in the *Institutes* on the definition we are examining, Calvin had insisted on this point, as though to forestall dismissal of the early part of his definition on the grounds that it seemed too formal or abstract:

> In understanding faith it is not merely a question of knowing that God exists, but also—and this especially—of knowing what is his will *toward us.* For it is not so much our concern to know who he is in himself, as what he wills to be *toward us.* Now, therefore, we hold faith to be a knowledge of God's will *toward us. . . .*

4. Faith is a *gift.* This is not merely a psychological insight propounded to protect mortal creatures from prideful asser-tions that they can create faith themselves or work their way up into God's presence by dutiful striving—important as those protections may be to a Calvinist. Rather, the recog-nition that faith is a gift is one of the consequences of the content of this particular kind of faith. A "benevolent" deity is one who offers himself freely, whose will toward us is good, who desires our well-being and therefore reaches out to us

even before we are aware of him. Calvin adds to the content of what we may already know of such a deity by telling us specifically that faith is "founded on the truth of the freely given promise in Christ," i.e., the grace which always is there first, so that while we can respond, we can never initiate. The most we can do is receive a gift. The same point is made in yet another way when Calvin tells that faith is both "revealed . . . and sealed . . . by the Holy Spirit." Here too the initiative remains with God. He offers the gift of his revelation and by his power enables us to receive it.

5. Faith is a *relationship*, involving the whole person. While it is indeed "revealed to our minds," it is also "sealed upon our hearts," i.e., given to the whole person. It is important that Calvin mentions both mind and heart in the same breath. Stress on the mind alone would reduce faith to dry intellectualism; stress on the heart alone would enlarge it to vague sentimentality. The gift to mind and heart confronts us with the giver of the gift and invites us to enter into living relationship with him.

It is important to see that relationship is possible only with someone who can be understood in personal terms. We emphasized in the preceding paragraph that faith is "founded on the truth of the freely given promise in Christ." But we do not enter into relationship with a "promise"; such a claim would make no sense. We must therefore inflect the same statement in a different way: faith is "founded on the truth of the freely given promise *in Christ*." The nature of this particular promise is that it comes to us in personal terms, in a life to which we can make response. It comes to us, more importantly, in a person *to whom* we can relate.

So Calvin. He too makes clear that faith is not simply a content to be learned but a commitment to be lived, and that it grows out of a reality of the past who (Calvin would insist on "who" rather than "that") can be appropriated in the present.

Two Working Definitions

It should be clear by now that these brief excursions into ways of using the word "faith" are converging in two directions, and we can distill from our discussion two working definitions, or at least descriptions, that will focus our subsequent reflections.

1. *Faith as the creative appropriation of an open past*

In all the instances we have examined, faith has had some kind of relationship to the past. Something has "happened" that must be put to some use. The lab technician does not start from scratch; there is a long history of experiments related to cancer research. He reflects upon them, follows up some that look promising, ignores others that lead in false directions. Sometimes he may have to start out in a completely new direction, but in no case can he proceed without taking the past into account. The sailor makes a judgment about the superiority of the compass to his own intuition, based on a long series of past experiences of the reliability of compasses and the fallibility of past intuitions, while the astronaut has worked long enough with "those guys back in Houston" to be sure that their judgments and expertise are so trustworthy that his very life can be entrusted to them.

Christian faith likewise stands in a special relationship to the past. Once again: something has "happened" that must be put to some use. There are enormous difficulties in trying to determine exactly *what* it is that has "happened," and some of these difficulties will engage us in the next chapter. We can only make a few provisional distinctions at the moment. There is an "event" (or more properly a cluster of events) centering around Jesus of Nazareth; there are a series of interpretations of the event, by Paul, Mark, Irenaeus, Anselm, Luther, Pascal, Schleiermacher, Rahner; there is teaching about the meaning of the event, in the form of doctrines such as incarnation, atonement, reconciliation, and so on; and there is an authority that determines which doctrines and interpretations are to be accepted as correct, such as a book or a tradition or an individual.

Now the problem is that although these distinctions can be made in a provisional fashion, they can never be made in a tidy fashion. When all is said and done we cannot talk about the event of Jesus Christ simply by itself; for we will always see that event through the eyes of certain interpreters, in the light of a body of teaching, and in terms of some view of authority that helps us choose *this* interpretation or *that* teaching rather than some other one. The danger, however, is that in this process we will get farther and farther away from any engagement with the event itself, and that we will substitute information *about* the event, or authoritative teaching *about* the event, so that the vehicles through which we can confront the event will eventually replace it. This is a truly absurd situation, which Kierkegaard likened to that of an individual who finally settles for a letter from his beloved as an adequate replacement for the actual presence of the beloved herself.

In our subsequent discussion of *what* it is from the past that we seek to appropriate, and (later on) what is the *content* of our appropriation, we shall have in mind as close an appropriation of the "event" as possible, bearing in mind that such an appropriation only happens through the mediation of interpretation, teaching, and authority, but bearing in mind also that to the degree that we concentrate too much on interpretation, teaching, and authority we are at an increasing distance from the basic content of our faith.

In terms of the example given in our initial discussion of the meaning of faith, Christians speak of "the faith once delivered to the saints," which is a transmission of teaching about the event. And they do something with it. They may decide to affirm it uncritically, or they may view it through a selective filter (the Reformation, existentialism, neo-Thomism, process philosophy), or they may repudiate most of it and start to rebuild in a fresh way, but in no case can they live and act as though the past were not important to them.

There is clearly no way we can escape our pasts, and part of the meaning of faith is what we do with them. The point would scarcely need emphasizing were it not for the fact that we are living in a time when many people, and especially the young, have become so disenchanted with the past and so skeptical of its value as to want to throw it overboard and begin all over again. They not only believe that "you can't go home again"; they have no interest even in making the attempt.

So it is *what we do with the past* that is important, as a brief examination of the controlling adjectives in our working definition should make clear.

On the one hand, the past to which we relate is described as an *"open* past." It is easy to see how people can consider the past as "closed": things, after all, happened, and they cannot be made to un-happen; they are done and cannot be un-done. But the assumption of "closedness" needs further examination. That Marx and Engels published *The Communist Manifesto* in 1848 is a given; that Jeshua bar-Josef was executed by the Roman state *ca.* A.D. 30 is also a given. But both of those events, though they happened in the past, are "open" in the sense that their possible meanings for us are by no means closed. New meanings can still be found that could make a difference to us.

The very interrelationship of the two randomly cited examples underlines the point. Until recently the two examples could have been contrasted by saying that the event of 1848 symbolized a claim that we must save ourselves, and that the event of *ca.* A.D. 30 symbolized a claim that since we ourselves could not bring about our salvation God had done so for us. But within the last few years much of the meaning of the *ca.* A.D. 30 event has been recast in the form of a discussion about whether or not Jeshua bar-Josef was a revolutionary, and whether or not his execution was a defeat of his revolutionary purposes or a paradigm of his revolutionary methods. Instead, therefore, of seeing these past events as "closed"—two diametrically opposite views of salvation—we now see that (whatever else they mean on other levels) they can shed complementary light on a common concern we have today, the nature of the revolutionary process, and that the past they encapsulate is thus still open.

On the other hand, our initial definition also described faith as "the *creative* appropriation of an open past." Our appropriation of the past cannot be a mere repetition of past words or world views. This would constitute a retreat from our present needs and possibilities that Arnold Toynbee rightly scores under the epithet of "archaism." Jürgen Moltmann gives a beautiful example of this:

> The church seems to live on memories, the world on hope. In theology one proves the truth by quotations from the Fathers; in the modern world by the success of experiments.

Not much is gained by giving a second-century answer to a twentieth-century problem, or by opting for Ptolemy's view of astronomy in a Copernican universe.

But let us not dismiss the past too hastily. It might be possible, for example, to see that both the second century and the twentieth century share some common problems, such as the question of what is the appropriate way for faith to respond to the totalitarian demands of a pagan state. An examination of various lines of resistance employed in the second century (epitomized in the book of Revelation or I Peter, for example) might provide models by means of which contemporary strategies of resistance could be measured. Properly understood and decoded, the book of Revelation becomes extraordinarily contemporary and is in fact increasingly important to radical Christians today. In a slightly different but analogous fashion, a contemporary examination of the patent clash between Ptolemaic and Co-

pernican world views might persuade contemporary astronomers that *no* world view is ever an absolute mirror of the
infinities of space it is seeking to understand, and thus keep
such astronomers from settling too complacently into the
interpretative model that is currently the accepted one. Thus
a *creative* appropriation of an open past is always possible
in a variety of ways.

2. *Faith as the dynamic interrelationship of content and commitment*

Samuel Hugo Bergman notes that the turning point in the
spiritual pilgrimage of the great Jewish thinker Franz Rosenzweig came when "he realized that his primary problem
was not to believe but *what* to believe; not whether to choose
faith but *what faith* to choose."

The statement poses a terminological problem that turns
out to be a theological problem as well. We have already
described faith as a *gift*, something offered to us which we
can receive, but not something we can engender or conjure
up. And now it is being suggested that faith is something
we choose, as though we initiated the process ourselves.

It is one of the oldest paradoxes in Jewish and Christian
history that on the one hand God initiates the relationship
to us and empowers us to respond to his prevenience (i.e.,
his coming-before), and that yet on the other hand a decision is demanded of us for which we bear full accountability.
There is no logical escape from the surface contradiction of
these two claims: if God chooses me, how can I be free to
make a decision? If I make the decision, how can God be
said to have chosen me? And yet there is a psychological
truth embedded in the paradox, that many religions, in addition to Judaism and Christianity, have recognized: I know
that I am confronted with a choice and that I bear the full
burden of responsibility for that choice; and yet in retrospect, once the choice is made, I also know that in some very

fundamental sense I was empowered to make it, and that it would be arrogant to take "credit" for it. In Christian terms, Paul saw this very clearly: "I, yet not I, but the grace of God in me"—such is the tenor of his message. And—even more boldly—on one occasion he puts the two realities side by side, issuing first the exhortation to decision and immediately putting it in the context of the divine gift that has made the decision possible:

> Work out your own salvation with fear and trembling; for God is at work in you, both to will and to work for his good pleasure. (Phil. 2:12–13.)

Whole books have been written on this problem, and to pursue it in detail here would be a diversion from our chief concern, which is to deal with the human side of the faith-relationship. To one who stands where a faith-commitment has not yet been made, the language of choice and decision is essential. To one who stands on the far side of that decision, the language of choice and decision is still permissible, for two reasons: (*a*) because decision is never once-and-for-all but always needs to be repeated and deepened, and (*b*) because the choice is still seen to have integrity, even though now, in retrospect, it is seen as encompassed by a power that enabled the choice to be made. In these terms, then, it is still appropriate to speak of "choosing a faith."

When we look once again at the statement about Rosenzweig, in the light of the above discussion, it should be clear that his problem is our problem too.

We cannot live in a vacuum. We are not confronted with a choice between faith or no faith, but with a choice between competing faiths—all of which (however else they are described) will have a content. We may choose faith in the power of human intelligence to solve all of its problems, faith in a world view that is deterministic or libertarian, faith in a political system that entails individual responsibility or that leaves it all to Big Brother, faith in a future that is either open or closed, faith in the God of Jesus Christ or the God of the Buddha.

So much should be clear, and the point needs emphasizing only against those who shy away from such a conclusion for fear that faith so understood will be reduced to "believing certain things," i.e., accepting propositional information, whether in the form of church dogmas or political ideologies. We can successfully overcome that hurdle by going on immediately to point out the necessarily intimate connection between content and commitment, between our view of "the way things are" and the resultant demands that acceptance of such a view places upon us. And the minute we get to this point there is another side of us that would prefer to retreat from such a conclusion, because it is the nature of faith so understood to make demands upon its adherents. A few examples will make this clear:

If (with John Calvin) we have as the content of our faith a belief in the God who acts in "divine benevolence toward us," i.e., if *He* is the nature of ultimate reality, then such a content demands from those who accept it lives that demonstrate a similar benevolence toward others—an uncomfortable and exacting life-style that most believers assiduously avoid.

If (with Dietrich Bonhoeffer) the content of our faith is a belief in Jesus as "the man for others," then such a content demands from those who accept it lives that are similarly oriented "for others"—an inconvenience at best and an unpleasant consequence at worst, particularly when the model on whom it is based turns out to have been crucified.

If (with Adolf Hitler) we have as the content of our faith a belief in Aryan supremacy, with its corollary that Jews contaminate the human race and should be exterminated, then such a content demands the creation of concentration camps to contain those who oppose extermination, and crematoria to carry out the exterminations themselves as efficiently as possible.

In each case, the cash value (as we say) of the content is determined by the degree of commitment of those who claim to believe the content—i.e., by the liveliness of the interrelationship between content and commitment.

This sort of conclusion is not just a homiletical twist put upon an otherwise academic discussion. What we mean can be indicated by our engaging in a brief linguistic inquiry into the meaning of faith. The Belgian Jesuit Père Louis Monden indicates that alongside the Dutch word *geloven*, which means "to believe," is the word *beloven*, which means "to promise," and even more significantly the word *zich verloven*, which means "to become engaged." The sequence suggests that to believe, i.e., "to have faith," is not only a matter of *believing something*, but also of *promising someone*, i.e., of making a commitment, most clearly spelled out by comparing the nature of the promise to the act of becoming engaged to be married.

Père Olivier Rabut, O.P., points out that the Hebrew root *'mn*, which gives us such words as "faith" and "belief," had, as one of its primitive connotations, the meaning "to carry a suckling child." The latter meaning (as he comments) illustrates as beautifully as could be done the faith which in its most basic sense implies both "benevolent care" on the part of the supporter, and "confident dependence" on the part of the one supported.

Thus is the circle closed between Dominican and Calvinist, for we remember that the content of Calvin's definition of faith was "the divine benevolence toward us," a counterpart to Rabut's "benevolent care," while the response Calvin wanted us to make to that benevolence was one of both "mind and heart," which is close to the "confident dependence" of which Rabut speaks.

Is There a Difference
Between Faith-in-general and
Christian-Faith-in-particular?

It might seem from the discussion thus far that there is a phenomenon called "faith" and that within this faith there is a subspecies identified as "Christian faith" which, like anything else, can occasionally be trotted out for illustrative purposes. There is an initial truth in this characterization that we must not miss. It is our strong contention in these pages that faith is not something limited to "religious" people (in a narrow meaning of that difficult word); rather, it is a quality of *every* human life, both in the sense of having a *content*, i.e., being a view of things, and in the sense of involving a *commitment*, i.e., involving an ordering of life in response to the content. As has already been pointed out, the real battleground is not the arena in which those who "have faith" compete against those who do not. Rather, it is the arena in which *competing faiths* do battle with one another for our allegiance. I see no way to avoid this reading of the human situation, I have no reason to wish to avoid it, and I will presuppose it in all that follows.

At the same time, such a reading of the human situation enables us to suggest that there are significant differences between faith-in-general and Christian-faith-in-particular, and also to clear up at least one remaining linguistic difficulty. To deal first with the linguistic difficulty: Some confusion is introduced because much of the discussion that focuses on the distinction between those who "have faith" and those who do not "have faith" is *not* in fact a discussion of faith-in-general but of Christian-faith-in-particular. In such discussions those who "have faith" are those who commit themselves to the God of *Christian* faith, while those who do not "have faith" are those for whom Christianity no longer is, or perhaps never was, true. Thus when

Hamilton, in the example cited in the Introduction, says that "the theologian today and tomorrow is a man without faith," and that we should "will this faithlessness," we can only presume that he is talking about *Christian* faith as something that is no longer a significant option for many persons. But such persons, Hamilton included, continue to live lives of faith in the overall sense in which we have been describing it, making commitments, responding to events, taking risks.

This suggests, in turn, several ways to take note of the difference between faith-in-general and Christian-faith-in-particular. The difference between competing faiths surely focuses *first* of all on the obvious fact that they have *different contents.* The statement "Whirl is king, having overthrown Zeus" is a faith-claim. The statement "In Christ, God was reconciling the world to himself" is likewise a faith-claim. Both indeed are explicitly theological faith-claims. The initial thing that distinguishes them is simply the fact that they have dissimilar contents.

The difference in contents immediately suggests a *second* difference (growing out of the second working definition developed above, which implied that different faith-contents will involve *different faith-commitments*), namely: there will be different kinds of responses. If Whirl is, indeed, king, having overthrown Zeus (i.e., if chaos rather than order is at the heart of things), then I may properly act chaotically, do whatever seems pleasing to me, and consider myself accountable to nothing beyond the whim of the moment. I can be sure that when I act chaotically I am being faithful to my view of reality. On the other hand, if in Christ God was indeed reconciling the world to himself (i.e., if healing love rather than chaos is at the heart of things), then I must act in a healing way myself. I must try to reach out in a healing way to those from whom I am separated, confident not only that this is the way my life is meant to be ordered but that, even when I fail in this attempt, the love which is at the heart of things will continue to reach out healingly toward me to empower me to try again. I can be sure that when I act healingly I am being faithful to my view of reality.

The difference between faith-in-general and Christian-faith-in-particular can be underlined in a *third* way by reference to our initial working definition of faith. We said that faith is "the creative appropriation of an open past." Faiths with different contents derive those contents in part by appealing (in what must initially appear as a very arbitrary fashion) to different normative events from the past. We will be pursuing this matter in more detail in the next chapter, so it is enough for now to give examples: the logical positivist views (or may view) everything in terms of the emergence of the truth that he sees embodied in the Vienna Circle of the early 1920's; the Jew similarly makes the exodus and Sinai normative; the Christian appeals to Golgotha and the resurrection; while the American patriot lives by an understanding of the American Revolution. All these positions are faith-stances; they are differentiated by the different events out of an "open past" to which they appeal for their authority.

There is a *final* sense in which faith-in-general and Christian-faith-in-particular are to be distinguished. The above considerations leave us with a claim (that other faiths would likewise make for themselves) that Christian faith is *sui generis*; Christian faith is unique and must finally be seen on its own terms rather than as merely one of a number of interchangeable faith-options.

This assertion is not as outrageous or imperialistic as it may sound on the surface, for it is merely an insistence that Christianity is itself and not something else, i.e., that Christian faith centers on claims that are made by it and not by other faith-claimants. There are certain things which Christianity shares with Judaism, for example, but certain other things that clearly differentiate the two faiths. The same thing is true of Christianity vis-à-vis Marxism. Those things unique to Christianity as a faith could be fully spelled out only by a full-blown account of Christian theology and experience. But for the balance of these pages our central concern will be with problems and possibilities raised within Christian faith. Some of the similarities and differences between Christianity and other faiths will emerge as the discussion unfolds.

The discussion may be brought into focus in the crucial distinction between Christianity and most other faiths. We noted it in Calvin's definition and it is a very important stress in the whole Protestant tradition. To anticipate a distinction developed in Chapter Three: when we speak of faith, what we mean is basically faith *in* someone, and only derivatively faith *that* something is true. To have faith *in* "those guys back in Houston" counts for more than simply faith *that* the instruments in the space capsule will function properly. It is relationship (i.e., reciprocity), in the first instance, that makes faith a constantly growing thing. Similarly to have faith *in* a God known to us in personal terms counts for more than simply faith *that* a world view makes sense. Once more, the first instance involves a relationship and a reciprocity that the second cannot supply. There is a *content* that is defined in terms of one to whom a *commitment* is made, and thus our two working definitions coalesce in the dimension of the *personal*.

Having described this as a particular characteristic of the Protestant tradition, we can fittingly conclude by illustrating it out of the Catholic tradition as well, and few Catholic theologians have put it as well as Fr. Joseph Ratzinger:

> The basic form of Christian faith is not: I believe something, but I believe *you*. Faith is a disclosure of reality that is granted only to him who trusts, loves, and acts as a human being; and as such it is not a derivative of knowledge, but is *sui generis*. . . . At its core faith is not a system of knowledge, but trust. . . . All the specific details embraced by

faith are but concretizations of the all-supporting movement of the "I believe in you"—of the discovery of God in the face of the man Jesus of Nazareth.

CHARTING A COURSE

The direction of our inquiry should now be clear. We have examined a number of contemporary and classical understandings of the word "faith" and have arrived at two working definitions: we have defined faith (1) as the creative appropriation of an open past, and (2) as the dynamic interrelationship of content and commitment. Our task is now to explore the implications of these definitions more fully.

In Chapter Two we will examine what it means to engage in "the creative appropriation of an open past," which is the problem of faith and history. In Chapters Three and Four we will examine the *content* side of faith as "the dynamic interrelationship of content and commitment," through an investigation of the problems of faith and knowing, and faith and doubting, respectively. Then in Chapter Five we will examine the *commitment* side of the same definition, exploring the problem of faith and doing. Since none of this is ever done in isolation, we will look briefly in the Epilogue at the relationship between faith and community.

CHAPTER TWO

The Uses of the Past; or, A Lonely Theological Corrective

(faith and history)

> Those of the left . . . want to abolish memory,
> those of the right . . . want to regulate it.
> —*Martin Buber*

DISDAIN FOR THE PAST

Putting in a good word for the past these days is a lonely business. Those who are not caught up in the "now" generation have their eyes fixed on a future that can scarcely be worse than what preceded it and might possibly be better. Theologians who decry backward-oriented tradition as baggage to be jettisoned, adopt a future-oriented hope as a liberation to be embraced, making only the most minimal obeisance to what lies behind. Alvin Toffler, in *Future Shock*, expresses his dismay at the way education looks backward instead of forward:

Every pupil in virtually every school, is carefully helped to position himself in space. . . . When it comes to locating the child in time, however, we play *a cruel and disabling trick on him*. He is steeped, to the extent possible, in his nation's past and that of the world. . . . The student is focussed backward instead of forward.

This contemporary disdain for the past was driven home to me in an interdisciplinary seminar at Stanford University in 1967, during the height of student activism and protest. The other professors and I had been foolhardy enough to prepare a list of suggested readings for the fall term. Our suggestions were received with scorn. The fault, we were told, lay not only with the particular books suggested, but with the very notion of using books at all. Even the most up-to-date books probably took at least a year to write, and another year to publish, so that by the time they got to the student they were hopelessly out of date. Mimeographed materials freshly run off might occasionally be permissible, along with a weekly sharing of personal experiences in forwarding the revolutionary struggle, but *books*? Hell, no!

As the year progressed, these and other students on our campus could be observed making almost every tactical mistake their forebears had made over the centuries in trying to advance the cause of social change, mistakes from which the reading of even a few books (all considerably more than two years old) might have saved them. I could not help being reminded almost daily of Santayana's dictum that those who ignore history are doomed to repeat it.

It was this experience, as much as any other, that forced me to begin thinking anew about the degree to which we depend on our pasts, and the present chapter certainly got its initial impetus from the confident rebuff of those dedicated but soon discouraged and ultimately disillusioned students.

FIVE CUMULATIVE THESES

We all have ways, then, of trying to cut loose from the past. But before we resolve to do so, it will be worth tallying some of the ways in which the past can act creatively upon us, rather than destructively. I propose, therefore, five cumulative theses that can amplify our initial working definition of faith as "the creative appropriation of an open past."

1. Merely on a descriptive level, it is true that *certain events from the past are normative for us, defining who we are.* A good many of these are "givens" over which we have no control, and they mold us in various ways whether we like it or not.

We have no choice, for example, about the date of our birth, a "given" that has immense effect on everything that subsequently happens to us, determining in advance whether we will live out our years in a technological or a primitive era, whether we will employ Spanish or English as our native tongue, and whether we will communicate with others via papyrus or television satellite.

We sometimes have a limited control over what we do with the "givens." During the lottery years of Selective Service it could and did happen that an American male born on August 17 (for example) might be drafted into the army on his eighteenth birthday and face the excruciating dilemma of whether to fight or resist the draft and go to jail or Canada, while an American male born twenty-four hours earlier or later might never even be called up for a physical examination, and might thus avoid the pain of having to face a far-reaching moral decision. In this example there is a "given," but those involved may be able to make a choice on the basis of what the given offers them.

While a birth date is not an occasion of choice, other dates *can* be chosen or rejected by us in such a way as to symbolize our attempt to define who we are. Thus 1776 has a special meaning for most Americans, just as 1789 has for the French, 1066 for the English and 1948 for the Israelis. But 1776 will have a different meaning to the English, and even to the American who views it from the perspective of the New Left rather than the D.A.R. The year 1789 will be remembered in varying ways in France depending on whether one is a royalist or a socialist, and 1948 will mean something quite different to the Arab than to the Jew. Similarly, the years 1861–1865 may have almost opposite meanings for those who now live above or below the Mason-Dixon line.

In the above discussion we are using dates as symbols of events, and we should remember that it is the events themselves that define who we are, even if the actual date has been forgotten or never clearly established. For increasing numbers of people in the Third World, the publication of *The Communist Manifesto* and the publication of the first edition of Marx's *Das Kapital* have become crucial events for understanding their own lives today, whether they know the publication dates or not. Those who stand in the Protestant tradition have their self-understanding similarly nurtured by the recollection of Luther nailing his Ninety-five Theses to the chapel door of the castle in Wittenberg, even if the precise date, October 31, 1517, is unknown to them, and even if some of the details surrounding the event should turn out to have been the embroidery of pious minds. For the Christian tradition, Jesus' crucifixion is a normative event, even though it is impossible to fix the precise date with accuracy. The Jewish tradition accords a similar centrality to the exodus from Egypt, an event even more difficult to date with precision.

2. In the light of this descriptive fact that certain events from the past are normative for us, defining who we are, we can take a second step by affirming that *such events have revelatory significance for us*. In self-conscious and selective ways we relate to certain events from the past in ways that help them *to give meaning* to who we are and what we do. They become "revelatory" for us in the original meaning of that word (from the Greek *apokaluptein*, "to draw aside the veil"). A new meaning can be found in present and future events when they are viewed in the light of certain past events.

We cannot draw indiscriminately on *all* past events. There are simply too many of them and our increasingly massive chronology would defy any kind of organization; we would be unable to make discriminatory judgments between the significance of event *x* and the insignificance of event *y*. We need some principle or principles of selectivity, some criteria by means of which to order our past so that it can have revelatory significance for our present and future. Consequently we choose certain events, initially rather arbitrarily, around which we fit other events so that new insight and direction and power can be drawn from them.

(We must, of course, recognize that the arbitrariness with which we choose is not totally capricious; we could almost say that some events are chosen *for* us, by virtue of our background, upbringing, previously determined values, and so forth. But in either case, certain events come to have immensely more significance for us than others.)

It is important to realize that the events we choose need not be *quantitatively* impressive to be *qualitatively* determinative for us. A single act of compassion may negate years of rebuffs and lead us to order our lives compassionately rather than cynically. Conversely, a single act of marital infidelity could threaten the trust that had been established over two decades, just as one act of selfless concern for the other could overcome the cumulative impact of years of debilitating relationship. The Jews make the single exodus event of deliverance the interpretative principle for a history that is otherwise chiefly comprised of episodes of bondage, rather than making the choice the other way around. Theologically, this principle can be expressed as the difference between *chronos* ("chronological" or clock time, in which all moments follow sequentially in undifferentiated fashion) and *kairos* (the "right time" or meaning-filled time, in which one moment can be normative for understanding all the rest).

Perhaps the best way to illustrate the point is by looking

more closely at the event just referred to, the exodus experience of the Jewish people, reenacted each year at Passover time in the Seder meal. What has impressed me most in the times I have celebrated the event with my Jewish friends is that this careful and detailed recalling of the past is never a device for retreating into the past in order to avoid the present, but it is always *a way of dealing with the past in order to give meaning to the present*. It becomes revelatory of what the present really is. Deliverance from the power of the Pharaoh is not only recalled but appropriated: past liberation becomes a foretaste of future liberation and is thus a celebration of new possibilities for the present. At the climax of the service it is said:

> In every single generation is it a man's duty to regard himself as if he had gone forth from Egypt, as it is written: "And thou shalt shew thy son in that day, saying, Because of that which the Lord did unto *me* when I came forth out of Egypt." Not our fathers only did the Holy One, Blessed be He, redeem, but us also He redeemed with them; as it is said: "And he brought *us* out from thence, that he might bring us in, to give us the land which he sware unto our fathers."

In the appropriation of these events, Jews can define and understand themselves as the people whom Yahweh frees.

This is particularly important when we observe that throughout most of Jewish history this would seem the least likely self-definition possible for the Jew. There have been many centuries of Jewish history when the here-and-now dimension of liberation was at best obscured and at worst totally lacking, when Jews were subjected to even more brutal bondage than that which they had suffered under Pharaoh. But it was precisely at those times that the memory of a past liberation could sustain them through a grim present toward the anticipation of a new future, and the reenactment of that past liberation in the Seder could fortify them to a new expectancy and even give ongoing meaning to a present that otherwise would have been utterly devoid of meaning. It is a matter of deep significance that the Seder has concluded for centuries with the cry of pain and yearning and hope, "Next year in Jerusalem!" To affirm, "Next year in Jerusalem!" is to see the past as a key to the future and thus to be enabled to work to transform the present.

The same exodus event has exercised revelatory power over other communities than Jews—an illustration of the fact that we can never limit or "close" the potential meaning of the past. Proponents of liberation theology (which we will be examining in Chapter Five) find their contemporary situation analogous to the situation of the Hebrews in Pharaoh's Egypt. Latin-American peasants and North American urban ghetto blacks, for example, are likewise in bondage, unable to control their own destinies, subject to the whim of those in power, demeaned and disfigured for the sake of their overlords. Both groups are finding in the "ancient" exodus story a paradigm of their own contemporary story and thus a description of new liberation possibilities for themselves.

In this retelling, new insights are emerging that have new revelatory power for the present. For example, it is being recognized that the liberation Yahweh worked for Israel was not only a symbolic freedom from the bondage of "sin" (conceived in personal and inward terms) but a freedom from oppressive and destructive political and economic structures. Built into the primal liberation experience is a recognition crucial for the contemporary liberation experience, the insight that "religion and politics *do* mix," and that contemporary ecclesiastical attempts to deny the mixing are a denial of the most basic tradition.

The liturgical appropriation of the exodus event by the Christian community offers a further illustration of how a past event can become revelatory for the meaning of present and future events. With local or denominational variations, every Christian celebration of the Eucharist exemplifies a creative interweaving of past, present, and future. The earliest account of the Lord's Supper, on which all subsequent liturgies are based, illustrates the point clearly:

> "Do this [*present*] . . . in remembrance of me [*past*]." For as often as you eat this bread and drink the cup [*present*], you proclaim the Lord's death [*past*] until he comes [*future*]. (I Cor. 11:25–26.)

The point is even more forcefully made if we adopt D. M. Baillie's instructive translation of *anamnēsis* so that Jesus' exhortation reads, "Do this *for my recalling*," i.e., in order to "call" the past event up into the present, so that it may become constitutive for the future. Something of the same sense of contemporaneity is achieved by the interpretation Daniel Berrigan insists should be given to the notion of "remembering," which means not only to think about something that once happened, but actually to experience "re-membering," i.e., being formed once again, having one's members re-created for the future.

Something important is being affirmed about the human spirit in the examples we have just used. We discover that people do not merely *talk about* events from the past that have revelatory significance for them, they *act them out*. Better still, they reenact them, so that the power they had in the past is repossessed in the present. This is surely the reason for the power of liturgy. It enables one to be a participant, to be *present* in what is held to be of unique significance, rather than being a disengaged spectator.

3. Such comments point toward a third way of seeing faith as the creative appropriation of an open past. To the degree that certain events from the past help to define who we are and thereby assume revelatory significance for us, *we shape our lives in conformity to the meaning of those events*. They become occasions of power as well as wisdom. They

not only reveal to us who we have been; they also challenge us to be transformed into what we can become. If we pose the question, "How do we use the time at our disposal?" an answer worth exploring is that we are to make the time at our disposal conform to the normative events of the past that have revelatory significance for us. Let us test this answer with four examples—one Jewish, one Christian, and two that are "secular."

As we saw earlier, for Jews to understand themselves as the people Yahweh frees seems unlikely if not grotesque in the light of Jewish history. One wonders, indeed, how Jews have managed to maintain hope, let alone survive, in the face of the psychic and physical annihilation to which they have so constantly been subjected. It is clear that a major reason for that double survival has been their recognition that they need not live only out of the destructive resources of the present or the indiscernible resources of the future. Rather, they can live out of the creative and discernible resources of the past, appropriating a normative understanding of themselves as the people Yahweh frees so that it defines their future hope and thus shapes their response to their present difficulties.

Once again the Seder meal illustrates the point, for it recalls and reenacts the exodus-Sinai experience that Will Herberg has called "the center of history" for the Jew. In their later history, Jews seek to make their present conformable to this event out of their past. If the present is a time of suffering, there can be a recollection not only that suffering has been the stuff of their history but also that in the midst of that suffering there is the promise of redemption from suffering. If the present is a time of relative liberation, there can be a recognition that liberation is always bought at a heavy price, that it is never historically secure, and that it could be replaced once more by bondage if the one who brought about the liberation, "Blessed be He," is forgotten.

Whatever the situation, it is possible to live out of the conviction that those who are in bondage can be freed, and that
the defining note of existence, even if it is momentarily absent, is liberation—a liberation partly realized in the present,
or hoped for in the future, because there was a liberation in
the past to which present and future are to be conformed.

In the Christian tradition, the comparable normative event
is Jesus' crucifixion and resurrection, which is a transposition
of the exodus-Sinai experience. Here, too, there is a dialectic
between suffering and deliverance. Christians, if living in a
time of suffering and anguish, draw strength from the affirmation that God himself, in some mysterious way, likewise
participates in suffering and anguish. For that event in human history from which Christians get the clearest insight
into the nature of what is ultimate is initially an event of
degradation and shame. As Christians experience their own
degradation and shame they discover that they are not cut
off thereby from God but rather drawn closer to him, since
that is where he already is.

That this is not just idle theorizing is illustrated by the
flesh-and-blood experience of Dietrich Bonhoeffer, a German
Lutheran pastor, who, imprisoned by the Nazis and ultimately executed by them, could affirm the divine compan-
ionship from his prison cell: "Only a suffering God can
help." At the same time, Bonhoeffer could appropriate the
fulfillment of the crucifixion episode in the resurrection as
not only a recital of the Christian past of others but as a
definition of his own Christian present as well. The testimony of his cell mates is that he lived as a captive who was
already free, giving strength to those around him, and going
to the scaffold unafraid, saying to a fellow prisoner standing
near, "This is the end—for me, the beginning of life." Such
creativity and hope were never superficially appropriated
(Bonhoeffer had earlier emerged as a militant opponent of
what he called "cheap grace") because the pain and the cost

were also a reality. But the pain and the cost were never the final word because the overcoming of the pain and the cost were also part of the past to which Bonhoeffer conformed his present.

A third example of making the present conformable to normative events from the past comes from a different tradition, the reception of *The Communist Manifesto* after its publication in 1848, and the encouragement it gave to dispossessed peoples in Europe (and subsequently elsewhere) to join forces because they had "nothing to lose but [their] chains." They were provided with a vision of a new kind of world—a world they could help to shape actively and creatively, instead of being shaped by it passively and destructively, a world that no longer needed to be dominated by greed or the overbearing power of the ruling classes, but a world in which each would give according to his ability and receive according to his need (a beautiful and "secularized" version, incidentally, of the vision of the Kingdom of God in the Jewish and Christian Scriptures).

Since the publication of that *Manifesto,* and what it has done to those who responded to it, there has been a century and a quarter for the development of political movements based upon it. Some of them have represented at least partial embodiments of the spirit it communicated, while others have obviously been false to its spirit and intent, Stalinism being a particularly clear example. The point is that present embodiments can be evaluated by the degree to which they advance or depart from the original vision. Here too there is a "usable" past that provides an ongoing vision for the future against which present embodiments of the communist ideal can be measured.

The example may be faulted (especially by Marxist "revisionists") for seeming to locate perfection in a static past and describing any deviation therefrom as a lapse or a "fall," and this criticism will be discussed later in the chapter. Before doing that, however, we will examine a situation in which the past is negatively normative, i.e., a past that must be repudiated in order to engage in a creative present.

Certain events from the past are so horrible that we must occasionally dwell on them in order to make sure we do not repeat them. We must, for example, refuse forever to blot out the memory of the Nazi concentration camps and crematoria that sent six million Jews to death in the 1930's and 1940's. After 1945, many Germans naturally enough wanted to "forget" this blot on their past, but ongoing recollection of it is the only way to ensure that its repetition never becomes a stain on anyone's future. Helmut Gollwitzer, a German theologian of that period, commenting on the later trials conducted by the German government to determine guilt for the inhumanity of Auschwitz, put it this way:

> Only if we are not easy on ourselves, only if we, each one of us, take ourselves to task, only if we look upon the *past* with open eyes, will we find the right path toward a *future* where repetition of such a past is barred and bolted out. And only then can we make full use of the opportunity the *present* holds for us.

If such a situation seems far removed from the average American reader today, a third of a century after the events it is describing, one need only comment that we Americans have our own analogues to Auschwitz—the death, maiming, and uprooting of almost six million southeast Asians, the callous disregard of even the most elemental "rules of modern warfare," the wholesale slaughter of civilians, the indiscriminate "carpet bombing" of vast areas of North Vietnam, and an unending list of similar atrocities that can be "justified" only by the grotesque moral calculus of complacency that the number slaughtered did not reach the Hitlerian equivalent of six million.

In the light of such realities, the problem is not that we

have been too engrossed with the past, but that we have forgotten it far too quickly.

4. Nevertheless, it is now time to confront a serious objection to our central thesis, the objection that such emphasis on the past, far from freeing us, locks us into a static view of life that immobilizes us. I shall first state the counterposition to this objection and then return to a consideration of the objection itself. The position I want to defend in a moment is that *conformity to normative events of the past is not bondage but liberation.* It is paradoxically by our surrender to them that we are truly freed for the present and the future.

Such a contention finds hard going these days. Many theologians are increasingly impatient with hearkening to the past, from radical Protestants who feel that the credibility of past events once normative has been forever destroyed, to Roman Catholics who fear that the massive upheaval in the church may discredit the reliability of the events that first brought the church into being. Young people, faced with a generation that has bequeathed them Vietnam, napalm, Watergate, Spiro T. Agnew, and the energy crisis, are understandably ready to cut their ties with roots that produce such unattractive fruits.

But an even more telling presentation of entrapment by the past is furnished in Elie Wiesel's short novel, *The Accident.* Eliezer, a survivor (physically at least) of the holocaust, who is now living in New York City, is run down by a taxicab on Times Square. It becomes clear as the book unfolds that "the accident" was one in only the most limited meaning of the word, for Eliezer had seen the taxi coming and had made no attempt to escape its path. We discover that he has been so destroyed by his past that he can take no creative approach to the present and future. While he is recuperating in the hospital, various friends urge him to "break" with the past, but it seems too powerful and destructive for him to be able to do so. The most he can come to is a decision to live a kind of creative lie, letting people help him, pretending to be grateful to them, but embodying no more than an ongoing deception. His artist friend, Gyula, who has been painting Eliezer's portrait in the hospital, finally engages in the dramatic symbolic act of destroying Eliezer's past by setting a match to the finished canvas and letting it be consumed before Eliezer's horrified and protesting eyes. But it seems that no less radical surgery can begin to free the patient from the destructive ties of his past.

This is not Wiesel's final statement of the matter, for he writes later novels in which genuine rather than spurious mutuality between persons begins to be achieved, most notably in *The Town Beyond the Wall*. But *The Accident* can stand as an ongoing rebuke to those who try too easily to establish creative ties with the past. We can note, however, some subsequent appropriations of the past by Wiesel that can be helpful in the present discussion.

First of all, we discover that while the destructiveness of the holocaust with its slaughter of six million victims is the source of Wiesel's anguish, in his later novel, A *Beggar in Jerusalem*, even *this* begins to have—retrospectively at least —a measure of redemptive possibility. The beggars discuss why Israel won the Six Day War, and one of them advances an almost mystical notion that the victory came because the Israeli forces had six million invisible but incredibly powerful allies, streaming from Europe where they had no graves, to help ensure a homeland for eternity that history had denied them in time. This is a notion needing much exploration, but it does suggest that even the most unredemptive events need not lock us totally into despair, for they can finally begin to work on us with a strange and liberating power.

Something of the same sort is happening in Wiesel's more recent novel, *The Oath*. The story is about a pogrom in central Europe in the 1920's, an ugly account of Christian vindictiveness toward Jews, in which the entire Jewish quarter of a town is wiped out—with the exception of the narrator, who has taken an oath never to tell the tale. Circumstances finally conspire to persuade him, half a century later, to break his oath. The reason for his decision is a conviction that to share the horror may persuade a young Jew of his acquaintance not to commit suicide. And so through this recital of the taking of life, another is persuaded not to take his own life.

In a third way Wiesel begins to appropriate the past creatively. In *Night*, his autobiographical account of Auschwitz, he describes in heart-wrenching terms how the sight of burning babies destroyed "forever" the Hasidic faith of his childhood:

> Never shall I forget those flames which consumed my faith forever. . . . Never shall I forget those moments which murdered my God and my soul and turned my dreams to dust. Never shall I forget these things, even if I am condemned to live as long as God Himself. Never.

Wiesel has, indeed, never forgotten, and he has devoted a quarter of a century to seeing that others do not forget either. But it is significant that after writing six novels to work through the holocaust experiences that "consumed [his] faith forever," Wiesel has now turned to a new literary genre. In *Souls on Fire* he is no longer directly telling his own twentieth-century story, but he is retelling the Hasidic eighteenth- and nineteenth-century stories, the stories that nurtured his youth, the stories out of his own past that it now appears were not totally "consumed" even by the fires of Auschwitz. However, to assert that Wiesel is no longer directly telling his own twentieth-century story is not quite accurate. He is, at least indirectly, telling it once again in a new form. For the old Hasidic stories are not just "old Hasidic stories," they are now Elie Wiesel's own story. They are his way of telling his story to the rest of us in such a way that they can become our story as well.

What at one time seemed an irredeemably destroyed past, a faith that had been consumed once and forever, now appears, a quarter of a century later, to be speaking with new power. If this can happen to even the slightest degree with the holocaust, the "extreme instance" of our times, then there are surely ways in which other events of the past can be appropriated with creative and liberating power.

Looking once more at two of the normative events from the past that we have been using as examples, we discover from our present perspective that they have often proved liberating rather than constricting. Jews, looking to exodus-Sinai, are defined by that event as the people Yahweh saves, and can thus dare to embody such a definition. Bonhoeffer, looking to the crucifixion-resurrection, could embody the same definition about himself. For the Jews, and for Bonhoeffer, there were sometimes insurmountable odds. The destiny of both is magnificently captured by Viktor Frankl, himself a survivor of the death camps, in the final sentences of his account of that survival, *Man's Search for Meaning*:

> Our generation is realistic for we have come to know man as he really is. After all, man is that being who has invented the gas chambers of Auschwitz; however, he is also that being who has entered those gas chambers upright, with the Lord's Prayer or the *Shema Yisrael* on his lips.

But there is another point to be made. A creative interplay can exist between the past and our continuing efforts to appropriate it, so that it becomes a dynamic and living past, rather than one that is static and dead. We have already seen how this can begin to be so in the case of Wiesel, but we can see other examples as well, particularly in situations *where we compare our appropriations with those of others*. I have, for example, a certain understanding of the American past. It has been formed in large part by the fact that I am a white middle-class Protestant, a child of the manse, who went to public school on the eastern seaboard and to college in New England. Those factors, whether consciously or not, have intruded into my selection of the events of the American past that help define for me what it means to be an American.

But I can no longer get away with that. For I am now bombarded with other and *conflicting* appropriations of the American past. Black history, for example, is now something of which I must preeminently take account. Until recently I never saw American history through black eyes, and if I am forever barred from doing so fully, at least I must now always observe how my white history looks through black eyes, and see what it has done to black people. That I do not like what I see is all the more reason for me to be forced to keep looking. The same thing is true in understanding the settlement of the West (where I now live) through exposure to the history of that same period as seen by the native Americans whom whites so mercilessly and murderously displaced, transplanting wholesale the techniques originally learned in displacing Indians from lands coveted by the Massachusetts Bay Colony.

Out of this kind of interchange, further enriched by the contributions of Chicanos, Nisei, Poles, and even Daughters of the American Revolution, come new ways in which the past can speak a liberating word to all of us as we escape from our parochial and therefore biased and self-serving appropriations of the past.

A certain restiveness, a recognition that we may have inadequately understood where we are, can also contribute to a reexamination of the past so that fresh insight about it can liberate us for the present. The classic instance of this restiveness is, of course, the detective story: a certain reading of the past, almost universally accepted, is questioned in ways that lead to radical alterations in all the characters' lives. H. A. Hodges has made the point vividly in comment-

ing on *Strong Poison*, a murder mystery by Dorothy Sayers.
There are two ways, he tells us, in which the evidence about
the murder of Harriet Vane's lover can be read. The first
way asserts: all the evidence in hand points to the fact that
she did the deed; therefore she must have done it. This is
the way the prosecution argues. But there is a second way
to read the evidence, and this is the way Lord Peter Wimsey
(who has fallen in love with Harriet Vane) argues: I am
sure she did not commit the murder; therefore "all the evidence in hand" cannot possibly be all the evidence there is;
there must be further evidence, and I intend to find it.

Which, in the manner of all good detectives, he proceeds
to do, conforming his present to a different reading of the
past from that of all the others, and thereby showing how
all the others have read the past incorrectly.

In a variety of ways, then, the appropriation of the past,
particularly if tested in the interchange of other appropriations, can provide a living past that is increasingly liberating
and energizing.

5. We can summarize our entire discussion about the
creative appropriation of an open past by insisting that *we
must maintain an ongoing interplay between past, present,
and future.* Truly to affirm any one of them means to affirm
them all: actually to deny any one of them means to deny
them all. W. H. Auden was surely overstating the case when,
in his legitimate desire to talk about the importance of the
present moment, he wrote:

> The past is not to be taken seriously (*Let the dead bury their
> dead*) nor the future (*Take no thought for the morrow*),
> only the present instant, and that not for its aesthetic emo-
> tional content, but for its historic decisiveness (*Now is the
> appointed time*).

Actually, the one who said "Let the dead bury their dead"
used the past to define who he was, citing the book of Isaiah
to describe his mission and then announcing, "Today this

scripture has been fulfilled in your hearing," (Luke 4:21),
while the admonition to "Take . . . no thought for the
morrow" actually reads "Take . . . no *anxious* thought for
the morrow," (Matt. 6:34), which is a very different thing.

It will not do, then, to isolate one (or even two) of these
moments of time at the expense of the others, and we must
examine the nature of their interplay. There are some illuminating examples in contemporary literature, and we shall
mention a few.

Gogo and Didi, Samuel Beckett's two famous tramps in
Waiting for Godot, seem to have the possibility of a future.
As the title of the play indicates, they wait. They wait in-
terminably. They return to the same place, day after day,
aeon after aeon. But *is* it the same place . . . or some other
place? And *is* it aeon after aeon . . . or only day after day?
They do not know. They cannot remember whether it was
this place or some other place, whether they were here (or
wherever they were) yesterday or long ago. *They have no
definable past.* And because they have no definable past, they
have no definable future: Godot might come and they would
miss him, not recognizing (i.e., remembering) who they
were looking for. Indeed, he may have come already and they
did not know it. And with no definable past and no genuine
future, it is clear that they have no true present; all they
can do is keep "putting in the time," hoping Godot will
come, but having no resources to draw upon during the time
of waiting.

Whereas Gogo and Didi have no definable past, Garcin,
Inez, and Estelle, in Jean-Paul Sartre's play *No Exit,* are in
precisely the opposite predicament. They have extremely definable pasts which they dredge up for one another in oppressive detail throughout the course of the action. What
characterizes them, however, is that *they have no definable
future.* Indeed, they have no future at all. The room in which
they are placed has "no exit," and we discover that this is
Sartre's stage definition of hell. They are condemned forever

simply to go through a meaningless charade of exchanges. The most they can do, once they are aware of their predicament, is acknowledge it. *"Eh bien, continuons"* ("Very well, let's get on with it") is the best they can manage. But since there is no future, no possibility of change, there is clearly no meaning to what is happening in the present and their pasts remain unredeemed as well, frantically appealed to, but powerless to deliver.

The lack of a definable future is not only a dramatic device. Simone de Beauvoir, who shared Sartre's life with him, confronts the approach of death and likewise realizes that in the ultimate sense she does not have a future either. This destroys for her what might have been the enduring beauty of the past and reduces the present to a cipher:

> I think with sadness of all the books I've read, all the places I've seen, all the knowledge I've amassed and that will be no more. All the music, all the paintings, all the culture, so many places; and suddenly nothing. . . . Nothing will have taken place. I can still see the hedge of hazel trees flurried by the wind and the promises with which I fed my beating heart while I stood gazing at the gold mine at my feet: a whole life to live. The promises have all been kept. And yet, turning my incredulous gaze toward that young and credulous girl, I realize with stupor how much I was gypped.

The revolutionaries about whom Albert Camus writes in *The Rebel* have yet a different problem. Whereas Gogo and Didi have no definable past, and Garcin, Inez, and Estelle (along with Simone de Beauvoir) have no definable future, the dilemma of the revolutionaries is that *they have no definable present*. Camus is morally incensed at the degree to which people, looking for a future free of hatred, bigotry, and violence, are willing, for the sake of that future, to consign the present to nothing but hatred, bigotry, and violence. They will sacrifice the present living generation ruthlessly for the sake of a future generation as yet unborn. They will justify suppression today in the name of freedom tomorrow, hatred today for the cause of love tomorrow, destructiveness today for the sake of creativity tomorrow. Everything they want in the future they are willing to deny in the present. So they not only turn the present into a jungle, but by doing so make the likelihood of ever transforming the jungle into a paradise extremely unlikely. Against such persons, Camus argues that "true allegiance to the future consists in giving all to the present."

Even that is not enough, as Robert Jay Lifton's study of the Chinese cultural revolution, *Revolutionary Immortality*, makes clear. It was not sufficient, the Chinese discovered, simply to give "all to the present." There had to be some assurance that the cause was worthwhile, that the present sacrifices would make a difference, that the revolution would finally succeed in its goals. In other words, there had to be an assurance of something analogous to the earlier belief in eternal life, a belief in what Lifton calls "modes of symbolic immortality."

We have seen some examples from contemporary literature of how things disintegrate when there is no creative interplay between past, present, and future. Let us now observe a literary character in whom the possibility for such creative interplay is more clearly present, Pietro Spina, the protagonist in Ignazio Silone's *Bread and Wine*. Nothing very spectacular happens to Spina in the novel. He is in hiding as it begins, he lives through most of the pages disguised as a priest, enjoying only a brief undisguised period in Rome, but is once again in hiding, and indeed fleeing from the police, as the book ends. Spina, however, is a prototype of what R. W. B. Lewis calls "the picaresque saint," one who, in a different milieu, comes close to the sanctity formerly reserved for the religious. What he achieves (in terms of our present discussion) is a creative interplay of past, present, and future.

Spina clearly has a *past*. He is a revolutionary who has

been a member of the communist party for many years. "Socialism," his old teacher had said of him, "was his way of serving God." It was also, one might add, his way of serving people. He returns to Italy, after many years abroad, during Mussolini's regime, and must therefore lead a clandestine life. Although he is ill and momentarily discouraged, he does have a past on which to draw, and it helps to sustain him.

Spina also has a *future*. He believes in his vision, which involves an ongoing identification with the peasants to achieve a better society for all. It is that vision of the future that caused him to forsake the *status quo* Catholicism of his youth and throw in his lot with the dispossessed. The disparity between that vision of the future and the present reality of the peasants has galvanized him into a life designed to overcome the disparity.

And this gives him a *present*. He has a usable past, even though he has sometimes been hurt by it, he anticipates an open future, and he uses the present for the sake of trying to overcome the tension between the two. He tells Infante, the deaf-mute, about a new world still to come, and thereby establishes communication with one who cannot hear him or speak to him, because he embodies the future he is talking about and thus makes it present.

But Spina's situation is never static. He must reexamine how past and future are related, when a disillusioned party member confronts him with the baleful challenge that in every revolution the oppressed become oppressors once they get power. And he must confront new possibilities in personal relationships for which his communist past had never prepared him, due to his priest disguise and the fact that people therefore approach him with a different set of expectations. Indeed, as the book ends, a young woman is sacrificing her life in an attempt to help him escape the encircling police net.

Many questions can be raised about the ultimate adequacy of Spina's vision (and some of these will be discussed in the next chapter), but we can surely see in Spina a style of "sainthood" we can affirm: because of what he learned from the *past* he has a vision of the future that informs the present; because of what is happening to him in the *present* he must continually reevaluate the past and draw new meanings from it for the future; because he can anticipate a *future* he lives in the present in such a way as to make creative use of the past. This is at least a model that other saints, less "picaresque," might well emulate.

Beyond the Past: Faith and the Future

Having insisted on understanding faith as "the creative appropriation of an open past," we may conclude by acknowledging that faith also has an orientation to the future and that this is another implication of our working definition.

We must note that the closest thing to a "definition" of faith in the Bible, the beginning of Hebrews, ch. 11, seems initially to undermine our entire discussion and point faith exclusively toward the future: "Now faith is the assurance of things hoped for, the conviction of things not seen" (Heb. 11:1). Fr. Joseph Ratzinger, whose perceptive study on *Faith and the Future* has already been employed, builds on this starting point, describing Abraham as one who "gave up the present for the sake of what was to come. He let go of what was safe, comprehensible, calculable, for the sake of what was unknown." This reflection on the faith of Abraham leads Fr. Ratzinger to conclude:

Faith is essentially related to the future. . . . It is a promise. It signifies the superordination of the future over the present and the readiness to sacrifice the present for the sake of the future.

The seeming discrepancy, however, between faith oriented to the past and faith oriented to the future is more apparent than real. For the reason Abraham could "give up the present for the sake of what was to come," is precisely that his choice was a response to the demand of a God he already knew, due to his *past* dealings with him. What Fr. Ratzinger describes as a faith "essentially related to the future" is exactly what is meant by liberation through the creative appropriation of an open past. Trust in what God has already done in the past makes it possible to trust in what he will do in the future.

Fr. Ratzinger himself, after emphasizing the future-orientation of faith, acknowledges the importance of the past-orientation as well:

> I maintain that reflection upon history, properly understood, embraces both looking back into the past and, with that as the starting point, reflecting on the possibilities and tasks of the future, which can only become clear if we survey a fairly long stretch of the road and do not naïvely shut ourselves up in the present.

It is noteworthy that the writer of The Letter to the Hebrews has hardly concluded his rather abstract definition of faith ("the substance of things hoped for") when he forsakes abstraction and starts talking concretely about faith by the use of specific examples, offering us a long historical recital, going back to the distant past, "the long stretch of the road" about which Fr. Ratzinger talks. Beginning with Abel, he offers example after example of the "heroes of faith." After moving from Abel to Abraham, Isaac, Jacob, and Joseph, through Moses and many more ("time would fail . . . to tell"), and describing what they went through ("Stoned . . . sawn in two . . . killed with the sword" and more), the author draws his conclusion, in a perfect example of what it means to engage in a creative appropriation of the past for the sake of the future so that a meaningful present will be possible:

Therefore, since we are surrounded by so great a cloud of witnesses, let us also lay aside every weight, and sin which clings so closely, and let us run with perseverance the race that is set before us, looking to Jesus the pioneer and perfecter of our faith. (Heb. 12:1–2.)

It will be in this tension of the open past, creatively appropriated for the sake of a vision of the future, that we will live out a meaningful present, a present in which we can begin to exemplify our second working definition, "the dynamic interrelationship of content and commitment," to a further understanding of which we must now turn.

CHAPTER THREE

Faith Within the Groves of Academe; or, The Possibility that Anselm Was Right After All

(faith and knowing)

> The human situation is distorted when a tension which belongs essentially to the structure of existence is resolved by distributing the elements in tension over two distinct classes of individuals.
> —*John E. Smith, disputing a division between "believers" and "nonbelievers"*

We have been cutting a wide swath in our discussion, and it is now time to focus on one of the consequences of taking seriously our second working definition of faith as "the dynamic interrelationship between content and commitment." We turn, therefore, to look at some of the implications raised by faith for the life of the mind. Can faith be an ingredient of the pursuit of knowledge by twentieth-century people, or is it simply an obstacle?

ACADEMIC HOSTILITY TO THE NOTION OF FAITH

We need not range very widely through contemporary writing to discover that if we call upon faith to enhance our understanding, we are likely to be looked upon with suspicion if not outright hostility. Surveys of intellectual history frequently portray the gradual emancipation of the human mind from confining servitude to faith and creeds, into the more ample realms of liberated reason, the open mind, and the spirit of free inquiry. In such assessments, the open mind invariably occupies the plus end of the spectrum, while the committed mind is at the minus end. To reintroduce a plea for faith and commitment, therefore, can only appear as a retrogressive step, bound to threaten our dearly won liberation.

If such a description borders on caricature, it does not unfairly distort the almost visceral reaction many intelligent people experience when confronted by the suggestion that faith can contribute to learning, particularly if the suggestion involves any special pleading by the religious establishment.

For this state of affairs the religious establishment itself must bear a large part of the blame. The story of the church's attempt to impose faith upon learning is far from a pretty tale, despite a few glorious chapters that can be woven into what on other occasions has been an ecclesiastical horror story. At its best, faith has encouraged learning; the university, after all, was initially nourished in the bosom of the church, and Gregor Mendel conducted his genetic experiments in an Austrian monastery. But the other side of the tale is a reminder of eras when free inquiry began to challenge hitherto unassailed theological presuppositions or philosophical first principles; then the shoe was on the other foot, and it was used to stamp out both inquiry and inquirer. The church's condemnation of Galileo is only the most celebrated in a long series of similar instances, and his recent ecclesiastical rehabilitation is a welcome though tardy acknowledgment of earlier institutional myopia. In more recent times, we have the sad tale of the church's unwillingness to let Père Teilhard de Chardin publish the results of his investigations for fear that the faithful would be disturbed, thus denying him the critique from scientific and theological confreres that would have enriched his writing even more. The result of such episodes has been that contemporary scholars insist on conducting their investigations without benefit of clergy and have fully established their right to do so.

This is not the whole story, of course. Certain scientists in Darwin's time, for example, Richard Owen, Ernst Haeckel, and Louis Agassiz, were initially more resistant to the implications of his position than were such churchmen as Charles Kingsley and F. J. A. Hort. There is also the remarkable story of the gradually increasing willingness of churchmen during several crucial decades to subject their own Scriptures to scientific scrutiny, illustrating a signal openness on their part to the importance of the life of the mind. But with whatever similar qualifications need to be made, it is still true that the intellectual community has had enough unfortunate experiences in the past to be suspicious of renewed attempts to bring about the remarriage of faith and learning.

The fault, however, does not all lie on one side, and if the insistence on faith has sometimes been imperialistic, the disavowal of faith on the other side has often been premature. The modern intellectual may be too ready to create a gulf between those who "have faith" and those who do not, and his assumption that the committed mind is closed off from serious inquiry is surely worth further examination.

Faith THAT . . . and Faith IN . . .

Can it be argued, for example, that faith underlies the whole intellectual venture, and that its presence is not only *not* a handicap to learning but a precondition of it? If so, it can be further argued that faith and learning, rather than threatening one another, are enriched and strengthened by a common partnership. To make the case, we must clarify, in this new context, our earlier distinction between faith as a content and faith as a commitment. We can do so in the following way:

Faith as a content is *faith that* something is true, for which the term *assent* has historically been used. In this understanding of faith, we give our assent to propositions or points of view such as the following:

The world is round.

God was in Christ reconciling the world to himself.

The music of Bach and Hindemith deserves serious
study.

Such assertions are very different in the nature of their claims, but they share at least this much in common, that we accept them, provisionally at least, on the authority of someone else. We do so without full verification or proof, and we can never be sure in advance that the proposition or point of view will turn out to be true.

Faith as a commitment, on the other hand, is *faith in* something or someone, for which the term "trust" has historically been used. In this understanding of faith we commit ourselves wholly and without reserve to the object of our faith, in such a way that we risk our very being in the name of that to which or to whom we have committed ourselves:

Though he slay me, yet will I trust in him.

I do promise and covenant, before God and these witnesses, to be thy loving and faithful husband, in plenty and in want, in joy and in sorrow, in sickness and in health, as long as we both shall live.

Martin Buber, in *Two Types of Faith*, summarizes the distinction in the following way, inverting the order used above:

We only know faith itself in two basic forms. Both can be understood from the simple data of our life: the one from the fact that I trust someone, without being able to offer sufficient reasons for my trust in him; the other from the fact that, likewise without being able to give a sufficient reason, I acknowledge a thing to be true.

It should already be clear that to whatever degree the "two types of faith" are separable for purposes of discussion, they are finally complementary and inseparable in the life of the person, and we must explore this contention with some care. An attempt to treat faith solely in terms of content would lack the dimensions of depth and involvement and (in Kierkegaard's meaning of the term) passion, suggesting the detachment of the thinker from the object of thought, while a treatment of faith solely as commitment or trust, without serious attention to the content of that in which trust is placed, would resemble what is pejoratively (and rightly) called "blind faith." Paul Tillich draws these two dimensions of faith together by defining the life of faith as one of "ultimate concern," meaning both that there is something that concerns us ultimately (content) and that our concern is itself ultimate (commitment). He suggests that no one is truly devoid of ultimate concern. Our object of faith is that which we treat with what Tillich also describes as "unconditional seriousness," that, in other words, for which we are ready to suffer and die.

Tillich's critics counter that many people are simply not grasped by ultimate concern, or at least deny the fact and have no desire to be described as possessing a concern they either passively ignore or actively disavow. Yet it can surely be argued that all of us have certain loyalties, certain criteria by means of which we choose to live (and perhaps even to die), which we have not "verified" in the ordinary manner of speaking, and yet upon which we stake the very meaning of our existence. As soon as we note that Christians have done so in terms of faith in the God and Father of their

Lord Jesus Christ, we must go on to note that others have done so in the name of different faith-commitments. Those in the groves of academe have assumed, for example, that truth is worth seeking for its own sake; that the universe is subject to orderly investigation and that the results of such investigation are trustworthy; and that it is better to be educated than ignorant. Human beings have also made contrary faith-assumptions: that truth should be sought so that it can be used to dominate other beings; that the universe is chaotic and that we can know nothing significant about it; and that powerful barbarism is preferable to impotent wisdom.

All these assertions involve faith-commitments. The notion that only those who adopt a theistic interpretation of the universe are having recourse to "faith" and that others are merely responding to "facts" is invalidated by the recognition that all views of the universe—whether theistic, monotheistic, dualistic, monistic, chaotic, or whatever—involve a content (assent) and, to the degree that the believer really takes the content seriously, commitment (trust) as well.

An illustration of the point can be found in an unlikely quarter—the sweeping attack on the very possibility of faith-utterances mounted in the famous first edition of A. J. Ayer's *Language, Truth and Logic*. Ayer's argument was that only *a priori* statements (i.e., tautologies) and empirically verifiable statements communicate any meaning. Statements that are not subject to empirical verification are, in the literal meaning of the word, "non-sense" statements. While they may tell us something about the emotional preferences of the speaker, they tell us nothing about the nature of things. Thus theological statements are nonsense, metaphysical statements are nonsense, and faith-utterances are nonsense, since none of them can be empirically verified.

Ayer, in his initial statement of his argument, asserted that "only empirically verifiable statements are true." He failed to recognize that this assertion was not itself an em-

pirically verifiable statement and that it was therefore pre-
sumably not true. A single unverifiable statement was being
used as a basis for destroying the integrity of all unverifiable
statements. Ayer, in short, was doing precisely what he ac-
cused the theologians and metaphysicians of doing, for his
attack on metaphysical speculation was itself an example of
metaphysical speculation.

Even the most sweeping critic of faith, in other words, is
liable to be hoist with his own petard. Everyone brings to
the life of learning a certain type of faith-presupposition that
has not been demonstrated in advance, that is not merely
the end product of cold, hardheaded scientific scrutiny, that
belies his stated intention to draw a hard, clean line between
"faith" and "facts." H. Richard Niebuhr makes the point in
more positive terms:

> The theologian finds many colleagues in the university who
> will not or cannot speak his language in whom the essential
> elements of what he calls "life in faith" are present. They
> practice, without confessing, a universal loyalty; they count
> upon the victory of universal truth and justice; they exercise
> a constant repentance, a *metanoia*, in self-examination and the
> search for disinterestedness; their scientific humility seems to
> have a religious quality.

Albert Camus exemplifies this kind of faith, especially in
The Myth of Sisyphus, The Rebel, and *The Plague.* Camus's
fundamental honesty is impressive. He rejects "consolatory
theism," for in looking at the universe he finds not meaning
but absurdity. The universe is deaf (*surdus*) to our passionate cry for meaning; absurdity is located in the gap between
that cry for meaning and the universe that will neither sustain nor answer it. And yet Camus, refusing to succumb to
such an order of things, calls the reader to join him in a life
of rebellious defiance, a refusal to condone "a scheme of
things in which children suffer and die." He opts instead for
a life of compassion, all the while recognizing an ultimate

victory of absurdity over compassion. He thus stands as a notable instance of the life of faith, not only in terms of a content ("Life is absurd") but just as powerfully in terms of a commitment ("I will defy absurdity and live compassionately, come what may"). Even if Camus had chosen the nihilist option, to which many of his contemporaries during and after World War II were attracted, that too would have illustrated the life of faith; it would simply have been faith with a different content and commitment.

The combination of content and commitment is likewise illustrated by the dedication of the contemporary communist, who not only commits himself to a faith, but also to doing whatever is necessary to exemplify the truth of that faith. The depth of this dedication has been documented in the moving account by half a dozen ex-communists of their initial faith-commitment and the gradual disillusionment and disaffection that followed. Their collective testimony appeared in a symposium with the significant title *The God That Failed*, indicating that the totality of their commitment had, as its only proper analogue, faith in God.

Our contention that "the life of faith" is participated in by everyone, and that it includes both content and commitment, may still fail to convince those who claim to be living life a day at a time, devoid of presuppositions or cosmic intimations. It may seem theologically imperialistic to insist that those who call themselves "nonbelievers" are in fact "believers," or that those who deny faith in one thing exemplify faith in something else by the very vigor of their denial. But it is still worth asking such persons why they make *these* decisions rather than those, why they opt to live rather than to die, why they think acquiring knowledge is important, why they accept some rules of society even as they rebel against others, why they oppose American foreign policy or support it, why they argue with such passionate moral seriousness that they are devoid of passionate moral seriousness. In all these areas, *some* covert form of faith-

commitment is surely present. Those who live by total whim
and randomness are rare indeed, and when they are apprehended it is usually for the purpose of putting them into
protective custody.

"FAITH SEEKING UNDERSTANDING"
—AND TAKING RISKS

If, then, the option is not between faith and nonfaith, but
between competing faiths, we can move to a further question: how does the life of faith relate to the life of learning?

In wrestling with this problem centuries ago, St. Anselm
spoke of "faith seeking understanding," and upon reflection
we discover that this is a fitting description of the whole
life of learning, whether Christian or not. The stance of faith
is not to be understood as one of insulation or isolation; the
stance of faith is precisely its reaching out for understanding.
Only if faith refuses to seek understanding, to take seriously
what it learns in that seeking, can it come under legitimate
indictment as a barrier to learning. The understanding that
is sought must have free reign and be able to pose all questions or challenges, however embarrassing or potentially
threatening. The process of faith seeking understanding is
thus laid upon all people without exception. Whatever faith
they hold—whether in the salvific power of Jesus Christ or
the scientific method or consciousness-expanding drugs—
must be a faith seeking further understanding.

The inevitable concomitant is *risk*. It is safer to leave faith
unexamined, for no one can bring faith out into the hard
light of public scrutiny, testing it in the face of competing
options, with any assurance of escaping unscathed. Cherished
items of belief may have to be put up for honest reassess-
ment, perhaps never to be recovered again, or at least not in
a form recognizably similar to what they were before the
onslaught. One's lot may even be to have faith demolished,

and to discover how searing it is to have to give one's own public accounting of "the god that failed." Whatever the content of the faith, then, it must undergo scrutiny, testing, challenge, and some form of *metanoia* (repentance) as it is refined and purified in the crucible of learning.

So just as all engage in "faith seeking understanding," all likewise embrace risk. Faith in a loving God may be shattered as we confront the rude and implacable reality of evil, and have to face the challenge of Camus's Dr. Rieux in *The Plague*: "Until my dying day I shall refuse to love a scheme of things in which children are put to torture." Faith in the saving power of intelligence may be strained as we discover the malevolent cruelty with which intelligence can be used to destroy people—intellectually, socially, psychically, and physically. Faith in social planning may be jolted by our discovery that planners can be bought and persuaded to plan to the advantage of the few rather than the many. A student's faith in the university as a haven of sanity and rationality in a mad world may be pushed to the brink by the discovery that intrigue and power plays are not absent from the campus any more than they are from city hall, or from defense-contract procurement. If we lay our lives on the line for those qualities which Jeremiah held to be more important than wisdom, power, and wealth—namely, "kindness, justice, and righteousness" (cf. Jer. 9:23–24)—we may have to reassess our reasons for doing so when we discover that the world treats those qualities cavalierly and cheaply. Faith that all knowledge and all conviction must be subject to empirical validation may be challenged by the discovery that we cannot account for the presence of "kindness, justice, and righteousness" by means of such a constricted vehicle of investigation.

The risk, then, is not one to which the conventionally "religious" person alone is subjected; it is a risk that engages everyone, the scientist no less than the theologian, as the physicist Werner Heisenberg makes clear:

If I have faith, it means that I have decided to do something and am willing to stake my life on it. When Columbus started on his first voyage into the west, he believed that the earth was round and small enough to be circumnavigated. He did not think that this was right in theory alone, but he staked his whole existence on it. . . . "I believe so that I may act; I act so that I may understand." This saying is relevant not only to the first voyages round the world, it is relevant to the whole domain of science.

Those who are reluctant to let faith seek understanding, those who accept without examination and who risk nothing, are not displaying firm, staunch, unyielding, invincible, or any other kind of faith. Rather, they are displaying an insecurity about the adequacy of their faith. Their timidity becomes a sign of unfaith.

FAITH AND ITS CONTENT

If faith is as central to the life of the mind as the foregoing analysis suggests, and if what we believe has significant consequences for what we do, then we must confront more directly the question of the content of faith and its consequences for learning. For what we are ultimately concerned about is not just "faith in faith" (as Will Herberg has described it) but faith in this god or that, this principle or that, this ideal or that. And it will make a difference what the choice is.

In the Biblical passage previously alluded to, Jeremiah urges us not to glory in wisdom or power or wealth, but to glory in the knowledge of a God who practices "kindness, justice, and righteousness," who delights in these things, and who expects us to exemplify them. But to offer such an agenda as the goal of the academic enterprise would immediately arouse suspicion if not hostility. What does this do to "the disinterested pursuit of knowledge for its own sake"?

Is this not to "use" education simply as a propaganda mill?

The suspicion must be countered by insisting that it is never enough just to talk about "learning." The crucial question is always, "learning *for what?*" If we do not seek "kindness, justice, and righteousness" and if we do not use the life of learning to enhance their appeal, we will—at least by default—be affirming something different from them. Not to promote justice is to run the risk of condoning injustice and perhaps being directly culpable in its spread. Faith and learning, in other words, are not neutral. If they are not proponents of one thing, they will be proponents of something else, and persons dedicated to faith and learning cannot indefinitely refuse to choose.

It is only the crudest illustration of the point to recall what the German universities became after the rise of Hitler, when a certain faith-stance took over the life of learning, when knowledge was transformed into a means of propagating Aryan supremacy and the eschatological vision of the Third Reich's reign of a thousand years. Much American education, at the other end of the spectrum, seems to be dedicated to turning out uncomplaining, upper-middle-class cogs in that consensus machine currently known as the Silent Majority. Faith and learning will not be neutral in such a situation. If the full life of educated people is to include a dissenting critique of majority positions, the position of the Silent Majority included, it will be a critique made from a certain faith-stance that implies decisions about what is important for society. If the criteria of Aryan supremacy or oriental supremacy, black power or white power, are inadequate criteria, what criteria are adequate? If the goals of "kindness, justice, and righteousness" are to be disavowed, then other goals must be avowed in their place, and the educated man may not avoid the necessity of grappling with what they will be.

Thus the *content* of the faith-stance is crucial. We have

already noted that the content of the Nazi faith produced the gas chambers and the crematoria, and that the faith was empowered by a fanatic conviction of its rightness. The faith-content of the culture that opposed the Nazis may have been formally "truer," but it lacked the power to produce a dynamic of revulsion until the horror had threatened to engulf the entire race. The issue, once again, was a battle between faiths, in which no neutrality was finally possible.

The previous paragraph may appear frenetic to middle-class Americans who do not believe that they face such momentous choices. Such an assessment, however, is possible only by middle-class Americans who are so overly protected from the revolutionary world in which they live that they are simply failing to discern the signs of the times. Educated persons who do not feel that their faith and learning compel them to take sides are living in a dream world, enjoying a luxury the real world will not much longer tolerate—a theme we will pursue in Chapter Five.

The issue on which we will be judged is not how much knowledge we have accumulated, but what we have done with it. My own sophomoric attempts to evade this truth in the early 1940's were forever laid to rest when I really began to internalize the fact that Hitler's propaganda minister, Josef Goebbels, had a Ph.D.

Faith as the Liberation of Understanding: Three Proposals

We can press the theme of "faith seeking understanding" still further by examining Anselm's other phrase, "I believe in order that I may understand." Anselm was not merely saying: "Since I have faith I must seek to understand." He was also saying: "Belief is the precondition of true understanding. If I am truly to understand, I must first of all believe." In so speaking he was echoing Augustine, who had elaborated a similar formula found in the old Latin translation of Isa. 7:9: "Unless you believe you shall not understand."

Whether we can be persuaded that belief is a condition of understanding, rather than a barrier to it, would seem to depend on the content of the belief. Some beliefs are surely barriers to further understanding. Clearly a belief that literal interpretation of every verse of Scripture is the precondition of true understanding can only be an obstacle to further understanding. Such a position rules out the evidential value of historical investigation, geological data, textual examination, the notion of secondary causes, and almost all the other tools that help us understand a text. But, by the same token, an insistence that no evidence counts unless it is empirically verifiable is just as dogmatic and circumscribed, and may cut us off from meanings that can be communicated by affection, string quartets, sculpture, tone of voice, or acts of sacrifice.

Certain types of faith, then, actually limit rather than liberate the mind. Partly for this reason, we cannot insist that a single methodology must embrace all realms of experience that "really mean" anything. Rocks cannot be understood in the same way as glands, and glands in their turn are not the only principle of interpretation possible for acts of courage or even courtesy. If Genesis is not a lens through which to view geology, neither is geology a yardstick for measuring the insights of Genesis. To make either one the norm for understanding the other is to distort Anselm's insight to read, "Since I already believe I no longer need to understand."

In what ways, then, can faith liberate rather than constrict the life of learning? We can suggest three ways in which this could come about: (1) faith can liberate us from inadequate understandings of the human situation; (2) faith as content can lead us to truer assessments of the human situation; and (3) faith as commitment can liberate us as total persons—heart, soul, and strength, as well as mind—to act in conformity with the degree of understanding we have been granted. We will examine each of these assertions in turn, using certain convictions of the Christian faith to illustrate each point.

1. We saw earlier that risk is inherent in the venture of faith seeking understanding. But traffic can go both ways on this street, and there is a similarly healthy risk involved on the part of understanding seeking faith. For just as learning offers a critique of certain types of faith, so faith can offer a critique of certain types of learning. The educated person, for example, who insists that the acquisition of knowledge is a sufficient guarantee of its proper use, needs the challenge of a faith that has learned with Jeremiah that "the heart is deceitful above all things, and desperately corrupt" (Jer. 17:9) and with Paul that "I can will what is right, but I cannot do it. For I do not do the good I want, but the evil I do not want is what I do" (Rom. 7:18–19). Otherwise, the individual may learn too late that there is no knowledge so pure or good that the human heart cannot turn it to evil ends. Conversely, the educated person who cynically views human relations in terms of nothing more than a slightly refined jungle ethic, needs to be challenged by a faith that insists that we are made in the image of God, that persons are of infinite worth, that love holds the central place in true human relationships, and that the highest form of love is the willingness to lay down one's life for one's friend.

In both cases, a particular perspective on the human situation is being challenged as inadequate. This does not mean that the faith from which the challenge is issued is therefore certified as adequate, but it does suggest that there are some things about a fully adequate perspective that are only learned through the risk of confrontation with faith. There is at least a possibility, as Reinhold Niebuhr often argued, that one faith may be able to do more justice to more facts than another faith, thus liberating the believer from certain false assumptions within which he might otherwise remain trapped.

2. The point can be put more positively by suggesting that faith as content can liberate the mind for a truer understanding of the human situation. The Christian, for example, affirms *the goodness of creation,* since it is the handiwork of God. Rather than foreshortening the life of the mind, such an affirmation can liberate the believer to an unfettered examination of everything within the created order. Few people have put this as well as H. Richard Niebuhr:

> Any failure of Christians to develop a scientific knowledge of the world is not an indication of their loyalty to the revealed God but of their unbelief. A genuinely disinterested science may be one of the greatest affirmations of faith and all the greater because it is so unconscious of what it is doing in this way. Resistance to new knowledge about our earthly home and the journey of life is never an indication of faith in the revealed God but almost always an indication that our sense of life's worth rests on the uncertain foundations of confidence in our humanity, or society, or some other evanescent idol.

There is no reason to fear what such investigation may uncover, for if this is truly God's world, the more we know of it the more we are enabled, in the words of the astronomer Kepler, "to think God's thoughts after him." Acts of investigation are acts of praise.

Faith that creation is not only good but also *orderly* can bring about a similar liberation. While this cannot be claimed as a uniquely Christian insight, having had a long history in Greek thought as well, it is an insight that was appropriated early on by Christian theology and it has played a significant role in its subsequent history. To affirm a faith in the orderliness of the universe does not necessarily commit one to a defense of the cosmological or teleological arguments for God's existence, but it does underline the point that one can investigate the world with a confidence that the results of the investigations will be trustworthy. It has often been remarked that the rise of modern science could only have come about in a culture permeated with a view of the universe as orderly and dependable, a view that Alfred North Whitehead traces to

> the medieval insistence on the rationality of God, conceived as with the personal energy of Jehovah and with the rationality of a Greek philosopher. . . . Faith in the possibility of science, generated antecedently to the development of modern scientific theory, is an unconscious derivative from medieval theology.

Had such a faith not been present, there would have been no reason to accept the cumulative evidence of repeated laboratory experiments as trustworthy evidence, and no reason to assume that the investigation of a universe characterized by chaos and randomness would produce anything save chaos and randomness. Behind the whole rise of natural science and empirical ways of thinking lies a faith in the orderliness of the universe, a faith that liberates the mind to the worthwhileness and the importance of such investigation.

Certain of the Christian affirmations about *human nature* can likewise be liberating rather than constricting. To believe that we are made in the image of God makes possible a confidence in the creative powers of the human mind and imagination that can unleash bold and venturesome experiments in thinking and living. At the same time, a realistic assessment of human sin makes possible a type of investigation that is neither Promethean nor Faustian, and which recognizes that our built-in biases provide a healthy safeguard against claiming too much for what we know. To believe that the self is fundamentally self-in-community, rather than individual or isolated self, can liberate us to realize that our knowledge is meant to be shared rather than hoarded, and that life lived solely in terms of individual self is quite literally self-defeating. To believe further that we are best described not by formulas or abstractions but by the life of

One who walked the earth himself—true man—thus providing a nexus for the commerce between God and ourselves, can liberate us to be receptive to truth that has already been offered to us, rather than limiting us solely to the discovery of such meanings as we can discern unaided.

3. When we seek to illustrate the liberating possibilities of faith as commitment or trust, we are moving into a different realm. For here we are not only describing the liberation of the mind but the liberation of the whole person— heart, soul, and strength, as well as mind. The life of the mind is not the whole of life, and the final test of faith is not simply the intellectual coherence it may provide, but the degree to which it empowers us to act on the basis of what we trust, i.e., "to stake our lives on it," as Heisenberg says. For someone to believe that the world is round, in a culture which affirms it to be flat, is not very compelling unless the believer is willing to risk falling off the edge of what his contemporaries believe to be a flat world. Faith does not work its full liberation until trust has joined in partnership with assent, until "faith that" coincides with "faith in"—i.e., not until there is a dynamic interplay between commitment and content. Socrates not only entertains the thought of death, he actually drinks the hemlock; Jesus not only asserts the trustworthiness of the Father, he actually endures the cross.

One of the clearest examples of such liberation is articulated by Martin Luther:

> And though this world, with devils filled,
> Should threaten to undo us,
> We will not fear, for God has willed
> His truth to triumph through us. . . .
>
> Let goods and kindred go, this mortal life also;
> The body they may kill: God's truth abideth still;
> His Kingdom is forever.

Luther not only had *faith that* God's truth was abiding, he also had *faith in* God to such a degree that he could stake his life on that belief in the most literal sense: "Let goods and kindred go, this mortal life also."

Dietrich Bonhoeffer, to whom we have already referred, is a contemporary example of this creative interplay between content and commitment. Bonhoeffer gave considerable attention to the rethinking of faith as content while he was waiting execution for his part in the plot against Hitler's life, and he made many bold assertions about the new directions that faith must explore in a "world come of age." Yet along with an intense intellectual preoccupation went a corresponding understanding of faith as commitment that enabled Bonhoeffer to live out his prison years with a remarkable freedom from anxiety or fear about the future, since the God *about* whom he thought was also the God *in* whom he trusted. The reality of this trust is captured in a prison poem written at the beginning of the last year of his life:

> By God's good power, miraculously given,
>   We wait with patient trusting, come what may.
> At evening and at morning God is with us,
>   And grants us fresh assurance each new day.

It was this faith that enabled Bonhoeffer to write, six months earlier, on the day after he learned that the plot against Hitler had failed:

> One must abandon any attempt to make something of oneself. . . . By this-worldliness I mean living unreservedly in life's duties, problems, successes and failures, experiences and perplexities. In so doing we throw ourselves completely into the arms of God, taking seriously not our own sufferings, but those of God in the world—watching with Christ in Gethsemane.

The liberation offered by commitment will not always be as spectacular as it was in Bonhoeffer's case. But that which his life and death exemplified to a supreme degree, the integration in a single life of content and commitment, is the possibility that is always open when we take with full seriousness the stance of faith seeking understanding. To hold such a faith is to believe that under its banner life is freed from fear and constraint. We still see through a glass darkly. We do not see all. But we see enough to trust that what we do not see is conformable to what we do. We further acknowledge that if what we do see is still distorted since seen through eyes of faith that remain sinful eyes, the further attempt to understand will help us repair the distorted vision with which we began. Thus there is no inconsistency, but even a necessary and appropriate consistency, in affirming simultaneously, "I believe in order that I may understand," and "I believe, help thou my unbelief."

Knowing, Doubting, Doing

These last reflections on faith and knowing have necessarily and properly begun to trespass on the theme of faith and doing, as if to remind us that no tidy division is finally possible. Before turning, however, to a fuller expansion of the relationship of faith and doing in Chapter Five, we must explore the challenge to faith that comes through the reality of doubt.

CHAPTER FOUR

The Struggle for Faith;
or, Faith for the Struggle

(faith and doubting)

> How can I believe in God when just last week I
> got my tongue caught in the roller of an electric
> typewriter? I am plagued by doubts. What if
> everything is an illusion and nothing exists? In
> that case, I definitely overpaid for my carpet. If
> only God would give me some clear sign; Like
> making a large deposit in my name at a Swiss
> bank.
>
> —*Woody Allen*

Woody Allen is spoofing. He knows it, and we
know it, and he knows that we know it. But the spoofing,
like the spoofing of a clown, is not far removed from pain.
There are many things we would like to laugh at that begin
to hurt when we look at them closely. Who has not echoed
the words, "How can I believe in God? . . . I am plagued
by doubts . . . If only God would give me some clear sign!"?
And while it may take more than a malevolent electric type-
writer roller to challenge our belief, and less than a Swiss
bank account to sustain our faith, we know very well that
faith and belief and commitment and trust are always vulnerable. Not only can they be challenged, they can be challenged with devastating effect.

Our hard-won affirmations are always subject to negation; the content we thought we had established is challenged by new data; the trust we had built up is nullified by a betrayal; the creative past that was once supporting collapses under the weight of evil; the death of a single child threatens the meaning of all other lives; a betrayal by a friend destroys years of mutuality and trust; a bombing raid nullifies belief in a God who cares for his creation.

There is no way we can live a single day without the possibility that doubt will threaten our faith. No examination of faith, then, can be complete so long as it sidesteps the problem of doubt.

WHY DO WE DOUBT?

Let us first of all distinguish between two kinds of doubt that are part of everyone's experience. The first of these has to do simply with our response to opinions or points of view: "I doubt that Hank Aaron will hit 800 home runs." This kind of doubt is relatively easy to handle: we can wait and see, we can examine evidence on the matter dispassionately, we can put the matter out of mind for long periods of time without any discernible loss of sleep.

The second kind of doubt, however, involves much more deep-seated apprehension or concern: "I doubt that we are going to be rescued from this life raft since we have already been adrift thirty-nine days," or "Because we all die, I doubt that God loves us." It is this second kind of doubt that will chiefly concern us in the pages that follow, a doubt that goes much deeper than hesitation or indecision or mere lack of information, and is much more readily described by such words as apprehension or even fear. These deeper ranges of doubt are helpfully symbolized in German: when one adds to the verb for "doubt" (*zweifeln*) the prefix *ver-*, which intensifies the meaning, the word that emerges is translated "despair" (*verzweifeln*). Truly to doubt, in our second meaning of the word, is to be close to despair. That Hank Aaron might not hit 800 home runs is not cause for despair (except, perhaps, to Hank Aaron); that we might not survive a shipwreck, or that all those we love are doomed, can indeed be cause for despair.

What things, then, cause us to doubt? Why do we so frequently find our faith assailed? Why can we not remain secure in the faith we have won at great cost and sacrifice? Let us explore five types of response to this series of questions.

1. We doubt because we are willing to grow

Frequently we doubt because we want to get at the truth of something and realize that there is more to know than we presently have at our disposal. Doubt, in this view, is an inevitable by-product of growth. Unless we are content to be intellectually and spiritually static, we must move in new directions, open up new avenues of exploration, remain discontent with what we presently know or are. We doubt because we care.

This kind of doubt is beneficent. It is the price of new insights, expanding horizons, and deeper commitments, and it is a price we pay with a high degree of willingness. This kind of doubt is a quality of the human spirit that leads to new advances and breakthroughs. Columbus doubted that the earth was flat. Beethoven doubted that the keyboard instruments of his day had reached mechanical perfection and wrote piano music that could only be played properly on instruments not yet built. Every scientific advance depends upon a scientist doubting that the conclusions of his predecessors are final, and acting on the basis of that doubt. The doubt can be costly, but most would agree that the cost is worth the pain. Dostoevsky, who knew this in a deeper sense than most of us, could say, "My hosannas have been forged in the crucible of doubt."

In Graham Greene's play *The Potting Shed*, a family has

been under the domination of an agnostic father who has tried to stifle all doubts from the lives of his wife and children. The family is spiritually destroyed until doubt begins to intrude, in the form of an alleged miracle that shakes their unquestioned agnostic assurances. "You've spoilt our certainties," is the way Mrs. Callifer initially responds to the extraordinary claim her son is making. But she actually welcomes the new state of affairs:

> It was all right to doubt the existence of God as your grandfather did in the time of Darwin. Doubt—that was human liberty. But my generation didn't doubt, we *knew*. I don't believe in this miracle—but I'm not sure any longer. We are none of us sure. When you aren't sure, you are alive . . .

"When you aren't sure, you are alive." Doubt can liberate, freeing us from old orthodoxies, whether Christian or (as in the case of Mrs. Callifer) agnostic.

One only gets beyond a static, or prematurely closed, or "blind" faith by entertaining doubt as to its present adequacy or ultimate finality. Only in this way does faith grow, mature, and deepen. Faith without doubt is dead. It is significant that Paul Tillich could say of his role as a Christian theologian, "Sometimes I think my mission is to bring faith to the faithless and doubt to the faithful."

2. We doubt because we fear that our faith is false

Not all doubt is beneficent. Most of it is threatening and grows out of a variety of fears. One of these is fear that our faith will turn out to be false. There is always the possibility of arriving at that fatal moment when we survey where we have been and are forced to the reluctant and devastating conclusion, "I've been had."

Reasons for belief that once seemed convincing begin to strike us as far less plausible than they formerly did, and the entire edifice appears threatened, a house of cards in imminent danger of toppling—not from some external gust of wind (a reason for doubt that will concern us later) but simply from its own inner structural deficiencies. Supports that formerly held it up appear worn out and there seems to be nothing firm to put in their place.

Clear examples of this kind of internal challenge are present in contemporary Protestantism and Roman Catholicism, in debates over the matter of authority (similar analogues could be found among contemporary Marxists or humanists). Both religions possessed, until relatively recently, clearly defined authority structures: the infallible teaching authority of the book in one instance, the infallible teaching authority of the pope in the other. The former authority is now widely discredited (at least in its traditional form) in all but the most closed-off bastions of Protestant Biblical fundamentalism. The latter authority is now widely challenged (at least in its traditional form) in all but the most closed-off bastions of Roman Catholic curial fundamentalism. In both cases, it is clear, the problem is the same: if an accreditation process for faith comes under question, can faith itself survive?

It is probable that both Protestantism and Roman Catholicism will survive these internal challenges to their authority structures and emerge from the struggle more solidly grounded than before, recognizing that faith can never finally be guaranteed by an authority structure, and that the only authentication faith can ever have will be a self-authentication based on commitment and risk rather than on externally imposed guarantees that make faith a "sure thing." If this happens, all of the present ecclesiastical trauma through which Protestantism and Roman Catholicism are going will be worth the strain.

The fundamental problem, therefore, is still deeper, and has to do with the internal challenges raised about the very *truth-claims* of the faith in question. Is it anything more than wish-fulfillment to affirm the forgiveness of sins? Is there any convincing reason to believe that the Buddha ever existed as a historic person? If the event of Martin Luther nailing his theses to the chapel door at Wittenberg is simply the embroidery of pious minds, have we not been deceived by manipulative people manipulating materials in order to manipulate us? If there never was a crossing of the Red Sea, what sense does it make to celebrate a non-event liturgically as though it had really happened? The questions are particularly poignant to those who stress the creative appropriation of an open past as we have been doing in the previous pages.

There are clearly no quick and easy answers to such questions, all of which need book-length discussions even to be adequately understood. The most we can attempt here will be a few pointers for ongoing wrestling with a problem that can never be fully and tidily resolved. (We will use the inner claims of Christianity as our example; limitations of space preclude our engaging in the same exercise with examples from other faiths.)

Our *first* responsibility is to be willing to face the problem head on. Faith-claims are not exempt from historical and scientific scrutiny, and it would be folly to try to keep our faith hermetically sealed against rigorous examination by contemporary scholarship. If truth is truly one, then the more knowledge we have, the closer we will be to the truth— even if some of our most cherished presuppositions are challenged.

To the degree that we open the truth-claims of our faith to this kind of scrutiny we can discover *secondly* that what initially seems threatening is sometimes both liberating and illuminating. The faith of an earlier generation was strengthened rather than jeopardized, for example, by the knowledge that the material in Isaiah, chs. 40 to 55, is from a different hand and historical situation than Isaiah, chs. 1 to 39. The information initially threatened a whole belief in how God works through Scripture, but its acceptance has proven creative rather than destructive. The power and the poignancy

of the latter portions of Isaiah, and thereby their meaning
for us, is enhanced rather than diminished when we learn
that the poems come from the difficult period of the Baby-
lonian exile rather than from "the year that King Uzziah
died." Their ability to speak with power to those in comparable situations of exile is thereby increased, and the contemporaneity of the Biblical message is enhanced. This is
but one example of the way in which there can be genuine
gains from a willingness to expose faith to an initially threatening critique.

We need to remember *thirdly,* however, that the inner
logic of faith-claims cannot be made totally dependent on
such a procedure. Historic or scientific scrutiny cannot become the sole or final arbiters of what faith is permitted to
retain and what it must discard. So to decide would be to
transfer, however subtly, our final allegiance to those who
were adjudicating the historic or scientific scrutiny; we would
have shifted the object of our ultimate allegiance to something else.

Here it will be helpful to recall our earlier distinction between faith as relationship to a person revealed in an event,
and subsequent reflection on that event in the form of interpretation, teaching, and authority. Our current discussion
focuses chiefly on interpretation, teaching, and authority—
for which we have been using the term "faith-claim," as dealing with the content of our faith. (Later in the chapter we
will be referring to a faith-stance, stressing the commitment
that faith entails.) As we have already insisted, we cannot
make a neat division between the two, and we will always
be making judgments about the event that defines our faith.
The scientist or the historian may do the same thing, and a
scientific or historical analysis may be able to tell us with a
high degree of probability *that* something happened or did
not happen. But this does not end the matter, it only begins
it, for now the way is clear for a discussion of *why* it happened, or the significance of its happening, and such ques-

tions as these (which are the really important questions) are not questions that finally stand at the bar of "scientific" scrutiny for their vindication, precluding the contribution that a faith-stance can bring to the discussion.

So it is not enough to be assured by historical research, for example, that there was no historical "Adam" in a specific location called Eden between the Tigris and Euphrates rivers at a datable time in the distant past. Such a conclusion does not end the discussion, it merely clears the way for the important discussion to begin: what does a story like the Genesis story say about how people in a given era understood themselves, their origins, their fears, their hopes, their relationship to what was ultimate for them, and how does such a story, so understood, illumine our understanding of our origins, our fears, our hopes, and our relationship to what is ultimate for us?

To ask the latter question as well as the former suggests a *fourth* thing we must remember, namely, that the "truth" about an event or a claim is found not only in what it is by itself, but in what subsequent use has been made of it. Many Christians, for example, claim to have been "saved" by Christ's death upon the cross. To the outsider, this sounds like a strange if not bizarre claim, something that surely has nothing to do with our own understanding of a historical event that occurred two thousand years ago. Even to many Christians today such a claim is difficult if not impossible to appropriate.

But before we dismiss out of hand the "truth" of such a claim, we need to remember that part of the meaning of the event of the cross is found in the fact that it has undeniably acted upon certain people in such a way that their lives were transformed by it. Such a statement as "The cross has saving power" at least describes what has happened to a great variety of people in a great variety of circumstances over the last two thousand years. We have not adequately described Jesus' death when we have said only that it took place on the city dump heap around A.D. 30, for such a description ignores the fact that that particular death has had a profound effect on subsequent history: Some people have themselves been willing to die in allegiance to the one who died there, and others (just to keep the record honest) have been willing to slaughter great masses of people who did not respond to Jesus' death in ways the slaughterers thought appropriate. The evidence is never fully in on the meaning of such an event, and the story continues to be written by each individual and each generation.

The example of Jesus' death suggests a *fifth* comment in response to fears that our faith may be false. There must be a historical kernel of truth out of which faith-claims spring and to which they respond, or else we can legitimately be challenged for holding a faith that is no more than wishful thinking, a "pretty story" that has no basis in fact or reality. It is surely a doomed faith that says only, "While there is admittedly no basis for these claims, let us live as if there were." We cannot indefinitely live our lives on the basis of an illusion or a deliberately contrived "helpful fiction." There is something in us that prefers truth to error, even though (as we shall see in a moment) we often look for ways to evade truths that are unpalatable to us.

No faith, on the other hand, can claim absolute assurance that events central to its story are fully authenticated, and in every faith some events have greater historical evidence in their support than others. That a man named Jesus died on a cross about A.D. 30, for example, is a reasonably well-attested fact with which few historians would seriously want to quarrel. The claim that Jesus walked on water, however, is quite another matter. His resurrection from the dead in three days is not subject to the same kind of historical investigation as the crucifixion "under Pontius Pilate," and his ascension into heaven is at a still further remove from such scrutiny.

While such gradations of potential verifiability may not

be particularly threatening to the believer, strong evidence that there never was any such man at all about whom such tales were told, surely would be. In the latter case, it would appear that the entire tale had been made up out of whole cloth, and one could legitimately feel victimized by the resultant skein of falsehoods.

Confronted with such problems, different persons will demand different degrees of "historicity" to assure themselves that they are not being led down the garden path, granting as a presupposition of subsequent reflection that no historical event can ever claim more than a relatively high (or low) degree of probability. Søren Kierkegaard put the demand for a historical kernel of truth at perhaps its lowest (or highest?) possible pitch, when he wrote in the *Philosophical Fragments*:

> If the contemporary generation had left nothing behind them but these words: "We have believed that in such and such a year God appeared among us in the humble figure of a servant, that he lived and taught in our community, and finally died," it would be more than enough.

For Kierkegaard, thirty-two words were more than sufficient, but such a bare-bones description would probably not do for many others. And yet, the matter is not finally one of quantity alone; thirty-two million words could fail to convince someone else. No words at all, however, would leave us utterly bankrupt.

Is there a way out of this dilemma? If there is, it is suggested by a *sixth* and final comment we can make on our overall problem: there is finally no "evidence" so coercive that it will force us either to believe or to disbelieve. Discovering whether or not we have been "had" is not something that just a little more evidence, or an ongoing open mind, will finally determine for us, though hard-headedness and a certain healthy scepticism are (as we have seen) essential ingredients in the life of faith. What will finally count decisively is the degree to which we feel that a faith-claim is important enough to entail risk on our part, so that the faith-claim leads to a faith-stance. Here Kierkegaard's likening of faith to "swimming over 70,000 fathoms" is an instructive image. The point of the 70,000 fathoms is to remind us that we cannot put our toe down and steady ourselves on the bottom before starting out. It reminds us that once we have begun we cannot have assurances guaranteed to us that the minute the going gets rough the ocean floor will be there to support us. The final vindication of our decision to enter the water will be: that we either sink or swim.

While a half dozen considerations do not dispose of our fear that our faith may be false, they may enable us to confront that fear more directly, and the very last response suggests another reason for doubt that we can now deal with more compactly.

3. *We doubt because we fear that our faith is true*

We doubt not only because we are afraid that our faith might be false; sometimes we doubt because we are afraid that it might be true. In this case, the threatening thing is not that we have hold of a faith that might slip from our grasp, but just the opposite: that our faith has hold of us in such a way that it will not let us slip from its grasp. Pascal saw the point clearly: "Why is it so hard to believe?" he asked, and then answered his own question, "Because it is so hard to obey."

Who wants to believe with Marx that the dialectic of history is on the side of revolution, if it means throwing oneself into the revolutionary struggle at great personal jeopardy? Who wants to believe with Luther that "A mighty fortress is our God, a bulwark never failing," if the consequence of such a belief is the exhortation, "Let goods and kindred go, this mortal life also, the body they may kill"? Who wants to become one of the "heroes of faith" that The Letter to the Hebrews describes when the catalog of such heroes quickly moves from those who "escaped the edge of the sword, won strength out of weakness" to those who "were tortured, . . . suffered mocking and scourging, and even chains and imprisonment" (Heb. 11:33–36)? Even when the challenges of the life of faith are less spectacular—involving simply the embarrassment of being laughed at for one's convictions, the nuisance of having to change one's life-style, the inconvenience of being shut out from one group of friends and having to find another—we find many reasons for wanting to evade it. There is no escape from the appalling possibility that the faith one holds is really true and that, if true, it would make inconvenient if not inordinate demands.

It is a widely noted psychological fact that the strongest resistances to conversion come just before capitulation. The most compelling arguments for nonbelief are always launched at such a time. The reason is not hard to find: to accept the new faith would entail a break with the past, perhaps an abrupt break, con-version, i.e., "turning about" in the most radical sense. Who wants to begin all over again?

Often the candidate for conversion is successful in mounting doubts of sufficient intensity to make possible a refusal of the new faith. It occasionally happened on campuses in the middle and late '60s that certain students and faculty were "radicalized" and brought close to the orbit of a revolutionary faith. Many backed off from final "conversion," some, no doubt, because they could not put the revolutionary claims together in a way that offered genuine hope for the future, but others because it was clear that a heavy price might be attached to such conversion—opprobrium, expulsion, the acknowledgment that one had been wrong in the past, difficulties with future employment, and so forth. The person in a similar stance of openness to Christian faith should beware of some similar costs also—the inconvenience of having to forgive one's enemies, the danger of affirming an allegiance higher than that demanded by the state, and so forth.

In the light of such demands, the potential revolutionary or the potential Christian (two terms that ought not to be mutually exclusive) can find plenty of reasons to decline full allegiance, or to withdraw from allegiances that had been given before all the implications were clear.

So stated, this reason for doubt might seem to be no more than timidity or even cowardice. But it can also be the product of a rugged honesty: "I see what the consequences of commitment might be, but I have no intention of fulfilling them and it would be hypocrisy to pretend otherwise. Therefore I decline the invitation."

4. We doubt because we fear that malevolence is at the heart of things

But there is an even more rugged honesty that lies behind the fourth and most pervasive reason for doubt. Doubt becomes real when we discover *a basic conflict between what faith affirms and what we see going on,* when our faith is challenged by realities and events that are destructive of that faith. This is clearest, and most devastating, when faith affirms goodness, but what we see going on embodies evil.

> Jews affirm their faith that Yahweh cares for his people —and six million Jews die in the holocaust.
>
> Christians affirm their faith that God has a purpose for every life—and a child suffocates in a crib.
>
> Marxists affirm their faith that on the other side of the revolution people will share their goods with one another—and after the revolution the oppressed become the oppressors.
>
> Humanists affirm their faith that people will respond creatively to rational argument—and slick propaganda

sways mass emotions in directions contrary to rational argument.

Americans affirm their faith in the integrity of the democratic process—and the single word "Watergate" encapsulates reasons for the disillusionment of an entire generation.

In each case, faith in something good is threatened by fear that malevolence, rather than goodness, is at the heart of things. The higher the "good" that is claimed as the interpretative center of the faith and the object of faith's allegiance, the greater the potential for doubt and despair when the faith content is challenged by what we see going on. In such cases the vision can not only fade, it can turn into its nightmarish opposite. In Camus's *The Plague*, Dr. Rieux sees Othon's child die horribly and must reject a plea by Father Paneloux to love what cannot be understood; one cannot love a scheme of things, Rieux responds, in which children are put to torture. All one can do in such a case is to set oneself against the scheme of things, work to negate it, and at least postpone its ultimate victory.

What we confront here is the problem, or (as Gabriel Marcel has put it), the mystery, of evil. All great literature explores it, all theology faces its greatest threat in trying to confront it, all faith is initially naïve and finally cruel that does not seek to cope with it. No brief paragraphs will suddenly dispel the mystery or somehow render the bad thing good, but (as in our previous sections) we must indicate some of the pointers that enable faith to grapple openly with this, its most ongoing challenge. Once again we will concentrate on the Christian faith as it confronts the challenge, since in no other faith is the conflict more acute between what faith affirms (love at the heart of things) and what we see going on (malevolence at the heart of things).

As we explore the conflict between *what faith affirms* and

what we see going on, we discover a number of possible conclusions to which we can come about this state of affairs:

a. We can conclude that what we see going on is in fact
the true reading of things, and that faith is thereby nullified.
This would be the view of non-Christians affirming that
some other faith-stance (Buddhism, humanism, or Marxism,
for example) offers a more adequate accounting of what they
see going on.

b. We can conclude that what we see going on is not in
fact a true reading of things, and that faith is thereby vindicated. This would be the view of triumphalist Christians who
impose a Christian world view willy-nilly, evidence to the
contrary notwithstanding.

c. We can conclude that what we see going on and what
faith affirms are both so seriously flawed that they must be
discarded. This would be the view of those who refuse to
ask the question seriously, asserting that nothing *is* going on,
that reality is an illusion, suffering is unreal, or something
of the sort.

d. Or, we can conclude that, in the ongoing interplay between what faith affirms and what we see going on, each
exerts an influence on the other; the Christian vision is
deepened by challenge, and what is going on is seen in a
different light when viewed from a Christian perspective. In
this ongoing interchange, the conflict between the two, while
never fully overcome, is reconceived and sometimes diminished, and what at first seem like opposite poles of a spectrum are brought into closer relationship, each helping to
illumine the other. This is the position we will briefly elabo-
rate in the following paragraphs.

Sometimes what we see going on does not coincide with
what in fact is going on. If I see two people fall off the
Golden Gate Bridge in quick succession, I am likely to report two suicides to the police. It may be, however, that
what was really going on was one suicide followed by an
unsuccessful attempt to prevent it. In this case, the first fall

was an act to destroy life and the second an act to save life. What I saw going on was not in fact what was really going on.

Suppose, however, that I was not only acquainted with both individuals, but deeply committed to them. I knew that one of them was going through a time of deep depression and had frequently spoken of suicide, and that the second had been devoting almost full time to helping the first recover a desire to go on living. In this case, my report to the police might have been quite different, and I might have suspected what actually happened. And as I later reflected on the whole episode, my initial estimate of the devotion of the second friend to the first would surely be heightened, for I would realize that there was present a dimension of caring even greater than I had initially assumed, in the form of a willingness to risk paying the ultimate price of laying down one's life for one's friend.

In this example there is a creative interchange between what I see going on and what my "faith" in my friends affirms about them. *Each enriches my understanding of the other, and each is changed in the process of the interaction.* Because of what I believe about my friends, my understanding of what I see is deepened; because of what I see, my appreciation of the depth of commitment of my second friend is likewise deepened. This does not make the events of the episode "good"; two lives have still been lost, both of them potentially full of much continuing worth to me and to others. But the congruence between what I see going on and what faith affirms about what is going on is at least a little greater.

We have enough resiliency to cope in remarkable ways with many of the disappointments, setbacks, and frustrations with which life confronts us. We can, if we so choose, usually bring a lot of good out of such experiences, "learn" from them, and all the rest. But the problem is of a different order of magnitude when we move to events from which little if

anything seems salvageable—terribly destructive and unde-
served evil; premature death; absolute denial of one's hopes,
dreams, and destiny. Even here, however, there can be an
interaction between what we see going on and what faith
affirms that can carry us at least partway into new possibilities. Let us look at the matter in its most extreme form.

Traditional Christian faith has asserted that God is both
powerful and loving. But what we see going on frequently
challenges either or both of those claims and almost always
challenges their being made together. If we affirm that God
is *powerful*, we find it hard to affirm that he is loving, since
so much happens in his world that love would never will;
whereas if we affirm that God is *loving*, we find it hard to
affirm that he is powerful, since love is so easily defeated. We
are left with the dilemma: if God is powerful he is cruel,
and if God is loving he is impotent. Such has been the classic statement of the dilemma.

Our previous comments can take us partway, but only
partway, through this thicket: some episodes that seem to
us defeats for love may not in fact really be so, and some
expressions of power that seem cruel may have more bene-
ficial results than we anticipate. But we are still left with
immense amounts of suffering and evil that cannot be so
explained. We must seek to explore more fully on this level
the possible interaction between what we see going on and
what faith affirms. And what happens as we do this is that
our previously held understandings of the meaning of divine
power and love undergo a transformation in the light of
what we see going on, and we discover that they are not
simply antithetical but can begin to be related in a new way.
We have to understand power differently. For in Christian
terms, divine power turns out not to be something static,
harsh, and remote, but something that can only be understood as *working through love*. And this in turn means that
we have to understand love differently. Let us see briefly how
this has been affirmed.

When we ask how Yahweh's power has been expressed in Jewish history, the answer is not that some celestial tyrant sat back and manipulated events through miracle after miracle in an implacable exercise of will, but rather that Yahweh wooed his wayward children, sought them in yearning and tenderness, made himself vulnerable to their rebuffs, and while he could indeed rebuke and judge them, when he did so it was always "judgment to save." He chose *not* to "execute [his] fierce anger" (Hos. 11:9), but to continue to reach out to them in love and to seek their freely given love in response. This was the way in which he exercised his power.

As the story is picked up by the Christian community, we find the Jewish claim being extended to embodiment in a man that Christians affirmed to be God present in their midst. And the sign of God present in their midst is, astonishingly, an instrument of political execution, a cross; the divine presence, however, is not embodied in the power of the executioner but in the powerlessness of the executed. The most vivid expression of God's love for Christians is a defeated man, suffering and dying on a cross. But—and this is the crucial thing in the present discussion—this expression of God's *love*, his suffering love, is also seen as the most significant manifestation of his *power*. This is the way, it is asserted, that divine power works: not by fiat, not by decree, not by a naked display of omnipotence, but through love. Divine power risks everything on the extraordinary gamble that it can elicit a response from those to whom it reaches out in suffering love.

What is happening here? What we see going on in the world around us challenges what faith traditionally has affirmed, and what faith has traditionally affirmed is therefore seen in a new light: power and love are understood differently from before. But the traffic goes both ways. For what faith *now* affirms about power expressed through suffering love challenges our view of what we see going on and forces us to see it in a new way. If what we have previously seen going on is defined by suffering, what faith now affirms about love is also defined by suffering, in the form of suffering love. And that, in turn, means that *we must see the suffering that goes on about us not as a place where God is absent, but as a place where he is present,* where he may in fact be most fully present, involved in it, participating in it, wrestling with it and unwilling to let it remain as it is, seeking along with us to bring some good out of it.

At the very least, what is going on and what faith affirms will now have this in common, which they did not have before: that there is an increasingly *shared* perspective about what is going on and what faith affirms, a perspective in which the God whom faith affirms is in the midst of what is going on rather than somewhere else.

This is not to say that the gap is ever fully closed. There are events in our world that it will never be possible to describe as good or as disguised expressions of love. That is why evil is a mystery to be lived with, rather than a problem to be solved. The death of a Vietnamese child by napalming, or of an American child by disease, or of an Indian child by starvation, can never be "justified" or somehow woven into a pattern that removes the sting, the anguish, the sheer defeat for love that such events represent. But what faith can affirm is that God is not aloof and uncaring, but is in the midst of just such situations as those, and that power expressed through love will always be the suffering love of identification, at whatever cost, with those in need.

Such a brief discussion does not begin to cope with all the questions and perplexities with which ongoing evil confronts us. But it at least sets a direction, and the very inconclusiveness of any "argument" forces us finally to realize that a time comes when argument ceases and we take a risk—the risk of affirming that, in the midst of much that remains unclear, the gap between what we see going on and what faith affirms is not totally unbridgeable, and that somewhere within the mystery of suffering love the best and truest hints and hopes are found.

5. *We doubt because we fear that indifference is at the heart of things*

The fear we most often express is our fear that malevolence is at the heart of things, that evil will overpower good. But there is another fear, perhaps less frequently expressed and perhaps therefore even more difficult to cope with, a fear that indifference is at the heart of things, that no matter what we affirm it simply doesn't matter. The challenge to faith is not that we will say, "I believe . . . ," and be confronted by a chorus on all sides responding, "You are wrong," but that we will say, "I believe . . . ," and be confronted by silence, or at best by a disinterested "So what?"

In some ways, indifference is more terrifying than malevolence. There can be a certain zest and challenge in doing battle with a known opponent, representing all that we detest, and there can even be a bittersweet pride in going down to defeat, knowing that we gave our all. But what if we are girded for battle and no antagonist appears or can even be located? There are times when it is easy to agree with W. H. Auden: "We are afraid/ of pain but more afraid of silence."

So the possibility that indifference is at the heart of things is a genuine reason for doubt. And since this fear has not received a great deal of attention in the voluminous literature on faith and doubt, it is important to explore the problem and see what kinds of responses can be made to it.

The doubts we have examined thus far, particularly our fear that malevolence is at the heart of things, seem to be posed for us chiefly because we are children of *time*. But the fear that malevolence is at the heart of things is enhanced by our recognition that we are children of *space* as well. Albert Camus writes in *The Plague* of a universe that is malevolent in the terms we considered above. But in an ear-

lier novel, *The Stranger*, he comments on "the benign indifference of the universe"—a universe that, even if it is not
hostile and aggressively out to get us, must be viewed with
apprehension because it simply ignores us, leaves us alone,
and is finally silent, uncaring and indifferent. This is the universe that, as we have previously seen, Camus describes as
"absurd," in the precise meaning of that term, i.e., "deaf"
(*surdus* is the Latin word for deaf, and *ab-* is a prefix that
intensifies the meaning of the word that follows). Absurdity
exists at that juncture where our "wild cry for meaning" is
met with no response at all, because everything around us is
deaf to that cry.

Suppose that appears to be our true situation. Suppose it
appears that we are simply "thrown" (the term is Heideg-
ger's) into a world that makes no provision whatsoever for
us and offers no response to our wild (or plaintive) cries.
Does this not write a cipher across all our efforts? If indifference is truly at the heart of things, faith is supremely
threatened.

And so our next question must be: are there any resources
that would enable us to see space as other than a threat, as
other than mere indifference, as something that could be at
least potentially beneficent? We will respond to this question through five pointers that will move us cumulatively in
the direction of an affirmative answer. The first two are insights from contemporary literature, while the last three
come from contemporary theology.

a. Ignazio Silone, in the preface to *And He Did Hide
Himself* (a stage version of the novel *Bread and Wine*, to
which we have previously referred), makes the comment:
"In the sacred history of man on earth, it is still, alas, Good
Friday." When Silone speaks in this fashion he is saying
something not only about history but also about the space
in which the historical drama is being played out, and he
conceives of space as potentially capable not only of sustain-
ing but of *nurturing* an ultimate meaning. For the title of

the novel in which Silone continues the story of Pietro Spina (begun in *Bread and Wine* and in *And He Did Hide Himself*) is *The Seed Beneath the Snow*, an imagery of seedtime and harvest. The space we presently inhabit may be covered with snow; it may appear to be uncaring and unresponsive to our need for sustenance and nurture. And yet, beneath the snow, unseen, unknown to those who walk over them, are seeds that may one day burst forth and blossom. Apparently uncaring space may become supportive instead of indifferent. Silone is telling us, in other words, that there is at least a potential coherence between the use we make of time and the nurturing of that use in the space in which we are set.

b. In a more unambiguously affirmative way, Georges Bernanos, in *The Diary of a Country Priest*, describes the space in which we live as beneficent. There is little in this novel to suggest beneficence, either on the part of space or time. The narrator is a poverty-stricken *curé* who has been notably unsuccessful, as that attribute is generally measured, and who toward the close of the novel is dying of cancer. Not only is his death imminent but he is going to die without receiving the most important possible bestowal of ultimate meaning on that death and life, the sacrament of extreme unction. But the priest has always lived, and is now prepared to die, in a context in which space is truly beneficent and supporting. When told that no priest can arrive in time to administer the sacrament to him, he makes the surprising and even scandalous remark, "Does it matter?" and then goes on to indicate why it does not matter, by saying, "*Tout est grâce*" ("All is grace"), which the English translator has beautifully rendered, "Grace is everywhere."

Now "Grace is everywhere" is an affirmation about space as well as time. It affirms not only that the deeds we do can be grace-filled but also that the context in which we do them, the space within which we find ourselves, can both support and nurture us. There is no place in which we are cut off from the possibility of the ongoing reception of a gift. There is nothing sentimental about this affirmation, as the priest's lengthy recounting of the obvious failures of his earlier life makes clear. But there is a positive appreciation of endless new possibilities in the context surrounding even our failures that is breathtaking in its simple profundity.

c. We can build on these literary clues by turning to a more explicitly theological treatment of our theme. As we do so, it is tempting to launch into an "ecology section," apparently almost a requirement for books in contemporary theology these days, but the temptation must be resisted, save to point out that it is our abuse of space that has led to some of our most horrendous human problems. As I bicycle to work on beautiful California mornings, amazed by the brightness of the sun on the green (and seasonally golden) contoured hills, I frequently wonder if we *deserve* the space we have been given, when I reflect on how we destroy those hills with "ticky-tacky boxes" for people to dwell in, or how we bomb the hills where other people dwell (always hills that are far from our own) and guarantee that for much of the human family space will remain a hell rather than a heaven or even an earth.

We can do many things with space: we can carve it in beautiful or ugly ways, and we can be creative or destructive in our appropriation of it. We have some control over it, but only some, and there are a few rules of the game we are not free to ignore.

It is quite conceivable, for example, that the created order is intended to be beneficent for us, provided we use it on its own terms rather than ours. We are "free" to defoliate the forests of Vietnam, and have done so with irresponsible abandon, but we have already discovered that this "freedom" was ill-used, since we have upset an ecological balance between forest, river, drainage, and vegetation cycles that may take hundreds of years to reestablish. Then there are all the homes, livelihoods, and human beings we have destroyed in the process, and there is the ill will we have reaped in Vietnam and elsewhere by our callous disregard of ecological nature and human nature in southeast Asia. The space we defoliated was clearly not *meant* to be defoliated, and our trespass against that elemental truth is already costing us—and the Vietnamese—dearly.

Similarly, there is an imposing rightness about the fact that if we befoul the atmosphere in our large cities by the smoke of our factories and the exhausts of our automobiles, we will gradually choke to death until we learn better ways of manufacture and transport. It is almost as if the space around us were exercising a slow but inexorable kind of judgment that can be creative if we heed it in time.

Perhaps there is a special meaning in Meursault's reference (in Camus's *The Stranger*) to "the *benign* indifference of the universe," and that its apparent indifference to our plight can lead us not only in destructive directions but in creative ones as well. If we will heed its warning, and read its signs aright, it could be "benign" in a sense Meursault may not have meant, i.e., filled with opportunities for favor and graciousness. An unrelenting warning, "This way lies disaster," confirmed to us when we try that way anyhow and are thereby led closer and closer to disaster, may be a warning for which we can finally be grateful. If, then, we are still called upon to "subdue the earth," we will have to do so in ways consonant with ground rules provided for us and not of our own making.

Such reflections may not lead us back to the "natural theology" of past eras, but they might lead us in the direction of a new "theology of nature." Needless to say, none of this is meant to deny what Tennyson called "nature, red in tooth and claw," or to suggest that there is something good about the capriciousness of a tornado swirling across the playground of a Kansas junior high school during the recess hour. But it is to say that there may be some ways to see a measure of beneficence even in the apparent intractability of space, and that in responding to its stern admonitions we could sometimes be healed rather than scarred.

d. A much bolder affirmation about space, and therefore a much more controversial step in the development of our argument, is found throughout the writings of Dietrich Bonhoeffer. Amid much that changes in Bonhoeffer's theology, there is at least one consistent theme throughout, and that is his emphasis on *structure.* As André Dumas points out in his incisive study *Dietrich Bonhoeffer: Theologian of Reality,* Bonhoeffer only infrequently speaks of Jesus Christ in the usual fashion as an event in history. Instead, his emphasis is almost always on Jesus Christ as the structure of reality. Consequently, it is spatial rather than temporal imagery that predominates in his discussion of the meaning of Jesus, and it is this spatial imagery that we must now seek to appropriate for our own use.

To speak of Jesus Christ as "the structure of reality" is to make a statement absolutely staggering in its implications, but it is the kind of statement on which any Christian contribution to our discussion stands or falls. For Bonhoeffer is not only saying (as do other theologians) that at a particular moment in time something happened to shed new light on previous and subsequent moments in time; he is saying that at a particular point in space the structure of all space is made manifest to us. On this reading, Jesus was not an intrusion into a reality totally unlike himself, but the one in whom the true structure of that reality has finally been made plain. The world is to be re-structured to conform to the nature of its true structure. So the universe is no longer malevolent or indifferent; it has a structure that can now be discerned, and, as Bonhoeffer goes on to point out, that structure is defined as—or, better, embodied in—deputyship, i.e., vicarious sharing in the situation and concern of the other, exemplified in Jesus as "the man for others." Bonhoeffer is insisting that such things as laying down one's life for one's friend, caring compassionately, "being there" for the sake of the other rather than the self, *do not defy reality but define it*. They are not intrusions or "sports" that go against the grain, they are one with the texture of the grain itself.

Bonhoeffer's conclusion can be related to our previous discussion in the following manner. To speak of Christ as an event is to make an appropriation from the past, and to speak of Christ as a structure is to have a content for the present, whereas to act on the basis of these two affirmations is to be making a commitment for the future, in which we take it upon ourselves to reshape, or as Bonhoeffer would say, restructure, our life and our world. Bonhoeffer himself insisted that this was the direction in which his thoughts pointed by noting that if Jesus Christ is indeed the structure of reality, the same thing must be true of the church that has dared to describe itself as his "body." If Christ is "the man for others," it follows that the church must be "the church for others," that structure in which vicarious living is the norm and not the exception. So Bonhoeffer defines the church as "Christ existing in the form of community," i.e., the "space" in which the true structure of reality as deputyship can be located. Re-structuring is (in Daniel Berrigan's phrase) "re-membering," being reconstituted, re-created as we were originally meant to be.

There are few today who would claim that such a description applies to any empirically identifiable church they see on the contemporary scene, yet the boldness of Bonhoeffer's vision must not be summarily dismissed. For he is insisting that not only can our life as creatures of time be given meaning but so also can our life as creatures of space. Just as certain moments of time can be normative for our understanding of all moments, so certain points in space can be normative for our understanding of all space. The structure of space, the *context* in which we live, is affirmed by this vision to be supportive of, and even to exemplify, certain values, chief among them being life lived for others. The true nature of reality is not described by malevolence or indifference. Rather, the true nature of reality is described by deputyship, and we can never finally know the one without the other. As Bonhoeffer put it in his *Ethics*: "I never experience the reality of God without the reality of the world, or the reality of the world without the reality of God."

e. It can be charged that the above discussion has artificially separated two aspects of our existence that cannot really be separated, i.e., time and space. Such separation can be justified only temporarily, for purposes of systematic discussion. In fact, however, measurements of space involve time (Arcturus, the fourth brightest star in the heavens, is thirty-six light-years away), and the experience of time occurs in space (from 1936 to 1952 Joe DiMaggio played center field in Yankee Stadium). Abraham Heschel spoke of his passionate belief in Judaism as a religion of time ("The Sabbaths are our great cathedrals"), but he could also say:

> To disparage space and the blessing of things of space, is to disparage the works of creation, the works which God beheld and saw "it was good." The world cannot be seen exclusively *sub specie temporis*. Time and space are interrelated. To overlook either of them is to be partially blind.

Karl Barth's massive treatment of the Genesis sagas, in *Church Dogmatics*, III/1, shows convincingly that from a Biblical standpoint space and time must be seen in relation to each other; there is a mutuality and consistency between them that forms a fitting coda to our discussion. In Barth's approach, the space-word is, of course, "creation," and the time-word is "covenant," the pact or agreement that Yahweh makes with his people. Barth distinguishes the two creation stories in Genesis by suggesting that the first (i.e., the priestly) account stresses creation or space, while the second (i.e., the Yahwist) account stresses covenant or time. The content of each illumines the content of the other.

The first story sees "creation as the external basis of the covenant": what is happening in the historic interaction between God and man, their covenantal relationship, is happening in a space that is created for the sake of that interaction. Space and time conspire on behalf of God's people.

The second story sees "the covenant as the internal basis of creation": the very nature of the space in which the covenant relationship is enacted is defined for us by the nature of the drama. Time and space conspire on behalf of God's people.

Space cannot be understood without time, nor time without space. A fuller understanding of one of them leads to a fuller understanding of the other. To the degree that time can be invested with meaning there is a corresponding possibility that space is invested with greater meaning too; when we receive a clue about the beneficence of space, time likewise is potentially more beneficent. Together, they conspire to give us hints and hopes (along with much that often seems to dim the hints and dash the hopes) that neither malevolence nor indifference is at the heart of things, and they leave us ever anew with the possibility that the heart of things is defined by love.

MOVING BEYOND DOUBT

None of it, of course, is ever a sure thing. There is no faith so secure that it cannot be challenged, no affirmation so serene that it is immune from attack, no conviction that has not been won by great struggle and maintained in continual jeopardy.

And yet, we do not simply live in the midst of doubt. To give doubt its due need not mean letting it always win the day. For even in the midst of doubt, we are always making affirmations with our words, but even more with our deeds. Even St. Augustine discovered, when he tried to be a total skeptic and doubt everything, that he could not really pull

it off; he had at least to believe in the truth of his own skep-
ticism, "I doubt," he was forced to conclude, "therefore truth
is." The very denial of truth is possible only on the assumption of truth's reality.

And even if to some that appears to be no more than a
verbal trick, it is at least a further reminder that we do make
some affirmations. We cannot wait until all the evidence is
in. All the evidence is never in. There is always more to
come, and there are no guarantees that it will all be supportive. Some of it may be threatening. We will continue to
amass evidence, sift it, weigh it, and finally adopt or discard
it, as long as we live. In that arena, the struggle between
faith and doubt is unending.

But there is something more to be said. For in the mean-
time we go on living and we do *in fact* continue to make
choices that are refining and deepening whatever faith we
have. We act daily in ways that indicate whether we are
opting for compassion or indifference, for love or for hate,
for persons or for things. The assurances to which we do
come will emerge as much if not more in the realm of action
than in the realm of thought. We vote with our feet, by
what we do.

When Jesus was asked why he should be listened to, since
he was not an educated man, he replied, "My teaching is
not mine, but his who sent me." And then, as if anticipating
the next question (i.e., But how can we be sure of that?)
he continued: "If any man's will is to do his [God's] will, he
shall know whether the teaching is from God or whether I
am speaking on my own authority" (John 7:16-17). In other
words, Jesus turned the issue back to his hearers. He did not
say: Here are three reasons to believe me, so that you can
be sure that I am right before you have to do anything. He
said rather that the only way to find out whether or not the
teaching was correct was to *live* it, with all the risks and
uncertainties that such a decision implied. Is love really at
the heart of things? There is no final answer to the question

short of responding: Try and see. Make love the normative principle of your life, expose yourself to those who have done likewise, and see for yourself whether your commitment to love makes sense or not.

Only by "doing the truth" (as the Fourth Gospel puts it) can its authenticity be established or denied. So the problem of faith and doubting is never finally resolved by another discussion or another set of arguments or a few more pages in an already long chapter on faith and doubt. It is resolved only by moving into the realm of faith and doing. We can emerge from the struggle for faith only by relying on faith for the struggle.

CHAPTER FIVE

Faith for the Struggle; or, the Struggle for Faith

(faith and doing)

> The encounter with God does not come to man in order that he may henceforth attend to God but in order that he may prove its meaning in action in the world.
>
> —*Martin Buber*

> [To be a witness] means living in such a way that one's life would be inexplicable if God did not exist.
>
> —*Emmanuel Cardinal Suhard, archbishop of Paris, during the Nazi occupation*

The reversal of the titles of Chapters Four and Five is not an attempt to be cute. It is intended to tie together two things that can never be separated—except when chapters get too long. The previous chapter led us to the conclusion that while *the struggle for faith* never ends, we deal with it most constructively as we use that faith for the struggle, immersing ourselves in the perplexities and decisions of ongoing life, confident that whatever degree of faith we possess will either be vindicated or further challenged when put to the test. We must now press the point home by recasting the theme and insisting that using our *faith for the struggle* is the most significant way to carry on the struggle for faith.

AVOIDING THE TIME AND SPACE TRAPS

We looked earlier at ways of using time and space creatively in the life of faith. There is a danger, however, that in so doing we will evade the thrust of the *immediacy* of faith, and use our spatiotemporal involvements as devices to avoid that immediacy and thereby escape the burden of demand that it places upon us. No one has exposed this danger more trenchantly than Martin Buber. He notes that we have an almost incurable thirst "for something spread out in *time*, for duration," a thirst that we try to slake by transforming God into an object of faith rather than the partner in a relationship. Faith, which initially (as Buber says) fills "the temporal gap between the acts of relation," is transformed into a "substitute for those acts," and instead of embodying the ongoing risk of relationship it becomes something we count on as a sure thing:

> The trust-in-spite-of-all of the fighter who knows the remoteness and nearness of God is transformed evermore completely into the profiteer's assurance that nothing can happen to him because he has the faith that there is One who would not permit anything to happen to him.

In similar fashion, Buber goes on, we have a thirst "for something spread out in *space*," and this thirst we try to slake by making God into "a cult object," one who can be located here or there and is at our disposal. Once again the immediacy of relationship is replaced, this time by ritualistic actions in special places. Faith is transformed into a quasi-magical device for the favorable manipulation of our needs.

How can we avoid these two types of temptation, and

use space and time in ways that will deepen rather than
atrophy our faith? Buber replies that the relationship of
which we have been speaking

> can be built up into spatio-temporal reality only by becoming
> embodied in the whole stuff of life. It cannot be preserved
> but only put to the proof of action; it can only be done,
> poured into life. Man can do justice to the relation to God
> that has been given to him only by actualizing God in the
> world.

It is to a consideration of this "doing," this "pouring into
life," this "actualizing God in the world," that our entire
argument has been leading us.

WORD TO DEED VS. DEED TO WORD

There are any number of ways to argue that faith must
lead to action, that action is the proving ground of faith, and
that what we affirm in our hearts or minds is not truly affirmed until it is translated into deed. Those who say love
and who live hate are not only denying their neighbors but
negating their affirmations as well. Better still, they are dem-
onstrating what their true affirmations are, when put to the
test.

In Arthur Miller's play *Incident at Vichy*, a number of
citizens in occupied France are arrested by the Nazi authori-
ties. The German Major in charge of the operation becomes
outwardly shocked at the way in which the "scientific" Nazi
doctor is exercising life and death authority over people randomly rounded up, solely on the basis of whether or not they
are Jewish. In an exchange with one of the prisoners, he says,
"I would only like to say that . . . this is all as inconceiva-
ble to me as it is to you. Can you believe that?" Leduc, the
prisoner, is unsparing: "I'd believe it if you shot yourself.
And better yet, if you took a few of them with you." The
Major offers all the conventional excuses for failing to act

on his professed belief: the dead Nazi scientists would be replaced by new ones, the prisoners who escaped would soon be rounded up, the whole thing would be an exercise in futility. Leduc presses him, insisting that the Major's presumed disgust means "nothing whatever, unless you get us out of here." If that is accomplished, he promises, "I will remember a decent German, an honorable German. . . . I will love you as long as I live. Will anyone do that now?" But something snaps inside the Major. His outwardly professed belief that anti-Semitism is wrong will not stand up when put to the test of risk-taking. In a matter of seconds his true faith is revealed, as he suddenly rants and raves about "goddamned Jews!" to the accompaniment of a flourished revolver.

The incident is instructive in many ways, not least for indicating that it often takes someone else to confront us with the kind of challenge that puts our faith to the test and insists that we act upon it. Two courses are open to us in such a situation, both consistent: either conform the proposed action to the professed faith ("I will help the prisoners escape because I believe Aryan supremacy is wrong"), or, failing that, revise the professed faith so that it conforms to the proposed action ("Actually, I do not really believe Aryan supremacy is wrong, so I will see to it that the prisoners do not escape"). In the case of the Major, the first course, which he repudiated, was honorable; the second, which he embraced, was dishonorable. There are, fortunately, incidents on record where the reverse was true: a German, outwardly professing the Nazi faith in Aryan superiority, came to a particular stress moment and hid or spared the Jew, defying orders and ending up in the concentration camp that had been created for his presumed victim. Such a one did not, in terms of the options outlined above, conform his proposed action to his professed faith, but took the second option, that of revising his professed faith to conform to what he actually did, even though he may never have verbalized the change. We can move from word to deed or from deed to word, and in the interplay we discover more clearly what our faith truly is.

This suggests a way in which we could put our own faith to the test today: by opening our professions of faith and our actions based on those professions to the scrutiny of others, and by learning from them whether or not there is any observable consistency between word and deed, deed and word. This might give us a much better check on the relationship between the struggle for faith and faith for the struggle than we can attain simply by self-scrutiny. The attempt, at any rate, is worth the effort. Whether it is worth the risk is something we can only decide afterward.

An Acid Test: "Liberation Theology"

As a case study in this illuminating and threatening procedure, we will examine an understanding of Christian faith that is gaining increasing support in the Third World—enunciated and practiced by many of those members of the human family who suffer extreme oppression, misery, and want at the hands of oppressors who are comfortable and affluent (the sort of people, in fact, who read and write books like the present one).

The position is usually called "liberation theology," and in order to understand its content we must first understand its context. The *human* context is a world in which 20 percent of the people control 80 percent of the world's resources, in which two thirds of the human family goes to bed hungry every night. It is a world in which the economic disparities between the rich nations and the poor nations are mammoth, in which there is a clear and ugly equation that goes: rich = white; poor = nonwhite. It is a world in which, despite occasional pockets of poverty in the former and pockets of affluence in the latter, there is a further equation that goes:

affluent, white nations = northern hemisphere; poor, non-white nations = southern hemisphere.

The *historical* context magnifies the poignancy of the human context. It describes a history in which for centuries the powerful rich minority has been increasing its power and riches through exploitation of the powerless poor majority, and a history in which, with very few exceptions, the church has been on the side of power and wealth, and therefore of exploitation. In a recent attempt to redress some of these imbalances, the United Nations instituted a "Decade of Development," during which special efforts were made to help the poor nations increase their economic capability, by loans and sometimes outright gifts from the rich nations. But the result of this effort was counterproductive. After the "Decade of Development," the gaps between rich and poor were greater than before. The story of our world today is that in relation to one another the rich are getting richer and the poor are getting poorer.

Consequently, the whole notion of "development"—the "trickle-down" theory of improving the imbalances by a certain flow of aid from rich to poor, is increasingly rejected by those in the Third World. They see it as (*a*) *paternalistic*, since it allows the rich to make decisions about what is "good for the poor"; (*b*) *manipulative*, since it forces the poor to dance to the tunes called by the rich; (*c*) *inadequate*, since it tinkers around the edges of a system supporting injustice, rather than challenging that system; (*d*) *repressive*, since it leads to unholy alliances between the financiers of rich nations and tiny oligarchies within the poor nations, both of whom have a vested interest in keeping the poor from challenging the arrangements that keep them poor; and (*e*) *deceptive*, since it does just enough to defuse concern that should be channeled into movements for genuine revolution instead of inadequate reformism.

It is in this situation of disillusionment with "development" that "liberation theology" has emerged, and we are now in a position to examine some of its chief characteristics. (In doing so, let us remember that although our discussion embraces the global scene, similar forces are at work on the American scene in the emergence of "a black theology of liberation," to cite the title of a book by James Cone, its most active proponent.)

1. Liberation theology not only grows out of the human historical context we have just sketched but out of a Biblical context as well. It is an attempt *to look at the world through Biblical eyes.* Its adherents see the Bible as a very revolutionary book, which is from first to last the account of Yahweh's liberation of his people. The exodus story is the paradigm event: Yahweh frees his people from oppression. The oppression is not just the oppression of sin, but the oppression of unjust social structures, enforced by a political tyrant and a repressive economic order. So the story is about political and economic liberation as well. The Old Testament prophets pound home the same theme, inveighing against corrupt judges, against the rich exploiting the poor, against religious leaders siding with the rich, against the few living in outrageous comfort while the many starve. Jesus stands in this same prophetic tradition; he too denounces exploitation, and proclaims a gospel of "freedom to captives" and "liberation to the oppressed" (see especially Luke, ch. 4). His story of the Last Judgment indicates that the nations (and not just individuals) are held accountable to God for whether or not they have fed the hungry, clothed the naked, taken sides with the oppressed.

So liberation theology asserts that in the vast labyrinth of Biblical materials, there is an "Ariadne's thread" to help us find our way out. The thread is the theme of God's identification with his people in order to liberate them, and his invitation to them to work with him in the achievement of that end. The Biblical God is a God who sides with the oppressed—not with the Pharaohs but with the slaves, not with the exploitative rich but with the exploited poor, a God who, when he becomes manifest in a human life, is found not with the wealthy or the powerful but with the dispossessed, the *am ha-aretz*, the poor of the land.

2. But the Biblical story does not merely illustrate a history lesson. It provides a picture of the contemporary scene. The Biblical account of the liberation of oppressed Israel is likewise a description of the possibility of the liberation of oppressed peoples today. If the God of the Bible took sides back then, it is clear that he continues to take sides today, identifying with the oppressed and challenging their oppressors. And this means that all who claim to believe in him and are trying to carry on his work *must take sides too*. Those who reject that conclusion usually argue that the church should not take sides; they ignore the fact, however, that the church has always taken sides in the past, but that it has almost invariably been on the side of the rich oppressors. The plea now is not that the church should take sides for the first time but simply that it should *change sides*. Having sided with the wealthy, it must now side with the poor; having been the support of those with power, it must now cast its lot with those deprived of power; having enjoyed privilege in the past, it must undergo risk in the future.

3. All of this means *a radical break with the status quo*, not only for those who take liberation seriously, but for the church as well. It is clear that the present economic and political systems will not tolerate, nor can they survive, the widespread changes that will be needed to bring liberation to the majority of the human family now being oppressed. Put bluntly, this means that capitalism is on the block, since its victims are persuaded that it will continue to treat them as objects and pawns in the power game for yet greater affluence and influence. Put still more bluntly, this means that the white nations of the northern hemisphere are on the block, too, and are being held accountable for their ongoing attempt to manipulate and destroy the two thirds of the

human family that is non-white, non-affluent, and non-northern.

4. It all adds up to *revolution*. The word sounds threatening to those who stand to lose in any radical break with the *status quo*, but it sounds liberating to those who have nothing to lose but their lostness. Proponents of liberation theology insist that revolution need not be violent. They insist that the decision about violence will be made, not by the oppressed majority, but by the oppressing minority that has the power, the guns, the money, the influence. If the oppressors will voluntarily share the superabundance of their goods, as the demands of love and justice dictate, well and good; but if not, then a more equitable sharing will have to come through the violent appropriation of what the oppressors unjustly possess and equally unjustly continue to accumulate. The present imbalances are intolerable. Rapid social change (which is really a euphemism for "revolution") is going to come. It can come violently or nonviolently, but come it will.

5. How, then, does one prepare for change? How do those without power get it? The process of working for change is called *conscientization*, the raising of the level of consciousness, perceiving the social, political, and economic contradictions in the society, becoming more and more aware of how truly repressive it is, so that action can be undertaken to destroy such structures and bring about liberation. In Latin America, the process of conscientization has been focused particularly in the peasant classes, and a "pedagogy of the oppressed," developed by Paulo Freire, has become a revolutionary method of teaching people that they need not remain at the mercy of their overlords, but that by thinking and acting together they can transform the world. Instead of teaching them to *accept* the present social system, as most education does, Freire's method helps them discover that they have it within their power to *change* the system. It is no wonder that both Brazil and Chile exiled Freire for the revo-

lutionary practice of teaching people to read and write. Conscientization is an intolerable threat to those who have power and are determined to keep it.

We can now see that liberation theology exemplifies the various characteristics of faith we have previously described. It is clearly an example of the creative appropriation of an open past, and it also exhibits the dynamic interrelationship of content and commitment, entered into at significant risk. Indeed, one of its most important contributions to our own understanding of faith is the extent to which a belief in Yahweh as Liberator leads to a commitment to enter with him into the task of liberation for all of Yahweh's children. Faith and action become virtually indistinguishable from one another; a key word is "praxis," reflection and action to transform the world. To believe in God is to believe that he is on the side of the oppressed, which means in turn that the believer must be on the side of the oppressed unless he wishes to deny his belief. The struggle for faith involves him in faith for the struggle. Faith for the struggle—involvement in the concerns of love and justice—vindicates the ongoing struggle for faith.

UNDERSTANDABLE RESISTANCES

Who wants to confront the impact of such a faith? Certainly not those of us who are the target of much of its polemic—affluent whites of the northern hemisphere. All it seems capable of doing is threatening us. It tells us that we are on the wrong side and that if we do not change sides things will be very rough for us in the future. But we immediately realize that if we *do* change sides, things will be very rough for us in the present. Those of us who are white middle-class Americans will be perceived as triple traitors—selling out our whiteness to the domination of dark-skinned peoples; acknowledging that our middle-class values are not only

empty but ugly, since they contribute to the ongoing oppression of others; and admitting that our nation is the purveyor of more violence and destructiveness than any other
nation on earth. Our "fellow Americans" (to adopt the most
exploited phrase of our times) do not take kindly to traitors.

If we take liberation theology seriously, we will have to
reexamine our jobs, since many of them, the minute we begin to explore their implications, will be found to be con-
tributing to the ongoing oppression of other peoples; we will
have to become uneasy with our affluent standard of living
as we recall that it is enjoyed in a world where 15,000 people
starve to death every day; and we will have to question the
whole fabric of our culture when we realize that those who
weave it stand on the broken backs of men and women who
are paid exploitative wages to produce the luxury goods we
don't really need. Here is a faith we want to doubt for fear
it may be true.

Who, in such a situation, wants to confront the full impact of liberation theology? No one. And so, quite understandably, we prepare a variety of resistances to it. Here is a
sampling:

1. "Liberation theology is trying to lay a guilt trip on middle-class whites. *I* am not standing on anybody's back and
it is unfair to accuse me of doing so. It's not my fault that
other people are oppressed. I don't have enough power to
oppress anybody, and what's more, I don't have enough
power to stop those with power from acting oppressively."

This is a legitimate rejoinder, and it must not be dismissed
too lightly. The difficulty with it lies in its overly individual-
istic view of who we are. Whether we like it or not, to be
white Americans in the latter part of the twentieth century is
to be part of that group in the world that has the most power,
influence, and affluence. The record is pretty clear that all
of those things are used for self-aggrandizement rather than
for the welfare of others. Of those who have much, the Scriptures inform us, much shall be required. There are still ways

within a democratic society that individuals, by banding together, can have an effect on policy, and no argument that totally disengages us from the actions of our nation is finally defensible.

2. "I object to the underlying premise that there is a clear dividing line between oppressors and oppressed, and particularly to the assumption that I must always end up as an oppressor. Latin American peasants and American blacks aren't the only people who are oppressed. We are *all* oppressed. Middle-class people are oppressed by middle-class values that lock them into the system, women are oppressed through their entire lifetimes by a male-dominated culture, white Americans are oppressed by the tax structure (unless they are millionaires or White House inhabitants who know the tax loophole game), students are oppressed by domineering young professors, young professors are oppressed by the tenure struggle. . . . Everybody is oppressed."

There are several difficulties with this argument: it is in danger of too easily trivializing and co-opting the term "oppressed"; it seems to imply that oppression can be overcome by relatively minor changes in the social order, and it conveniently locates the oppressors somewhere else than in our own vicinity so that the heat can be taken off us. It is a bit like equating the magnitude of harm done to two persons, one of whom is tapped by a flyswatter while the other is being run over by a bulldozer. To the degree that the argument contains some truth, however, we will pick it up again later in our discussion.

3. "What you have presented as 'theology' is nothing but a thinly disguised version of Marxism. It is a this-worldly faith, preaching class struggle, the overthrow of capitalism, and the triumph of the masses through the use of violence. It is not Christianity but communism."

There is no doubt that Karl Marx is taken more seriously than Adam Smith or even John Kenneth Galbraith, but the appropriate response is not to make Marx mendacious, but to determine whether the description furnished by liberation theology is or is not an accurate portrayal of the world in which oppressed peoples find themselves. Marxism can be an analytic tool of considerable help without necessarily being the answer to the questions it raises. That some of the things Biblical theology long ago affirmed on its own terms turn out to have resonances with contemporary Marxism does not invalidate the Biblical insights, and this is a matter about which Christians have often been overly nervous.

4. "Liberation theology seems to think that only by some vast social engineering project can life be made tolerable for most people. But in the past, rich nations like our own didn't get rich by socialistic schemes. They got that way by hard work and initiative. Why can't poor nations today do the same thing? The cure for poverty is work, not handouts."

Here we confront a complex issue, not resolved either way in a matter of a few sentences. The difficulty with the argument is that it assumes nonexistent analogies between past and present. It is a totally different matter for a poor nation to become economically viable in today's highly competitive trade markets, compared to achieving national prosperity a couple of hundred years ago, when there was still an almost limitless American frontier, and when nations that were powerful but not economically self-sufficient could exploit the raw materials of their colonial subjects and increase their power and wealth at the expense of others. Today those "others" are caught in the economic and political bind that such a history has imposed on them, and they do not have the options that were available to their colonizers. So the response remains too simplistic.

5. "Liberation theology is a distortion of the faith it purports to proclaim. Christianity brings about reconciliation while liberation theology glorifies conflict. Christianity puts the individual in relation to God, while liberation theology is only concerned about relating individuals to one another."

The reconciliation-conflict debate is a difficult conflict to reconcile! The danger in the position stated is that reconciliation will be sought, not through the facing of conflict, but through the pretense that conflict does not exist. True reconciliation, however, can come only when tensions, polarities, and conflicts have been brought out into the open and recognized for what they are. This is, of course, initially threatening, but any talk of reconciliation that does not take account of it is not the reconciliation of two parties but the subjugation of one party by the other. Advocates of both liberation theology and the position represented above need to remember also that Jesus said that the second commandment (to love the neighbor) was the same as the first (to love God). There is no legitimate way for any expression of Christianity to separate the two.

There are surely other arguments that could be mounted, and still further responses that could be given to the arguments already mounted. But at least some of the points of tension are now before us. If there is any common denominator running through them all it would seem to be that of resistance to change, a resistance we can call "understandable," since those who have it made are not eager to have their lives unmade. In such situations, fear may sometimes replace logic, and maintenance of the *status quo* may become more important than facing facts.

But those who take seriously their membership in the Christian community have to face, however fearfully, the fact that liberation theology is voicing a genuine concern felt by many within that community. Those of us who continue to resist the message must face the possibility that our own perception of our faith has been so strongly conditioned by our being white, middle-class Americans that in the process we have seriously distorted it. We must be open to the possibility that there are some new things to which we need to listen.

Is There a Transfer Value?

Let us assume that there are a few who will try to listen. Let us even assume that we are among such persons and that we believe that liberation theology is telling us some things that in the blindness of our own affluence we cannot see without its help. It will then be impossible to conclude that liberation theology is simply meant for some other situation. We will have to ask about the transfer value of such a theology to *our* situation. Can a theology for the oppressed also become a theology for the oppressors?

Those who have forged a liberation theology in situations of great oppression are the first to raise questions about its transfer value. They rightly fear that if the oppressors take over their themes, or even their terminology, liberation theology will be co-opted and defused of its power. (This has happened even within the Latin American scene, where a repressive Chilean government ostensibly took over the method, and actually took over the terminology, of Paulo Freire's "pedagogy of the oppressed" and subtly transformed it into an instrument of social repression instead of social liberation.) White northern "liberals" often talk rather romantically about "liberation" and "revolution" and "consciousness-raising" and even "violence," and yet manage to do so in ways that do not threaten by one iota the social, political, and economic structures in which their hearers live. We should not expect therefore that we have built bridges of understanding when we have aligned ourselves verbally with liberation theology. We may, in fact, have created new barriers of alienation.

Such lack of ability to communicate across cultural, class, and racial barriers, was devastatingly illustrated at a conference in Geneva in May 1973 on "Black Theology and Latin American Theology of Liberation." Two Latin American theologians and two black theologians (one from the United

States and one from Equatorial Guinea) spoke to a group of about sixty participants, mainly from Europe. So diverse were the backgrounds and vested interests of all concerned that communication was virtually impossible, not only between the four speakers and the Europeans, but even between the black theologians and the Latin American theologians. The experience was discouraging, but it was also salutary, for it made clear how futile it would be to assume premature agreements that will actually crumble under the weight of even cursory analysis.

Black theologian James Cone put the point with appropriate sternness toward the end of the conference: "I do not believe that the oppressed and the oppressors can communicate at levels where it really makes a difference, because they have different realities to which the symbols and the language refer." But not even Cone could quite leave it at that, and in a later comment he opened the door at least a crack:

> Since I am a Christian and I believe in the work of the Holy Spirit, one has to be careful about the limitations one places on the Spirit. In mysterious ways I would have to conclude that many things are possible . . . even the possibility of Europeans—white people—understanding what oppression means to black people.

Accepting as a hard reality that black theologians and liberation theologians are going to be rightly suspicious of those who imagine that they can "identify with the oppressed," is there any way to keep the channels open and begin a response? I believe that there are a few things that can be addressed to those who hope for an affirmative answer to the question:

1. The first thing we can do is indicate our willingness *to listen* and be ready to listen for a long time. This is hard for people who have been used to taking the initiative, assuming leadership, and expecting others to snap to attention. Europeans and North Americans must be ready to live with the

fact that leadership in the future, theological or otherwise, is not going to come from Europeans and North Americans but from Asians, Africans, and Latin Americans. Those who have been used to offering answers must now be content to ask questions, willing to learn from those who until very recently were assumed to be the perennial pupils. (Parenthetically—or should it be stated in boldface print?—it must be emphasized that we must listen to Third World Christians at first hand. We may not settle for second-hand reports, even in books called *Is Faith Obsolete?* Moral: Let no one feel that he or she has mastered, or disposed of, liberation theology on the basis of the discussion in this chapter.)

2. As we listen, we must pay liberation theology the respect of *taking it seriously*. There is an easy put-down to positions we prefer to avoid: we call them "fads." But no theology that is articulating the hitherto-unspoken concerns and aspirations of a majority of the human family, those who Frantz Fanon called "the wretched of the earth," can be written off as a "fad," a movement that will soon run its course, as have such movements as the "death of God" and even the "secular city." We must assume on the contrary, that the impact of liberation theology will widen and deepen, and that it will not fade away until widespread oppression fades away, which, even on the most optimistic of calculations, will not occur for many decades.

3. As we listen seriously, we must acknowledge that liberation theology is a *genuine Christian theology* and not a contrived importation.

As even the brief exposition above makes clear (second-hand though it be), liberation theology is telling the Biblical story and insisting that the Biblical story is also a contemporary story. To be sure, it is not the only way the Biblical story can be told, and those who are telling it will freely acknowledge, when challenged, that the telling is influenced by the situation of oppression in which the tellers find themselves. But they go on to insist that since Israel's story is itself the story of an oppressed people, it is more likely to be accurately translated today by those who are also oppressed peoples than by those who are among the oppressors.

4. As we listen seriously to this genuine Christian theology, we need to recognize that not only does it describe a situation somewhere else, but that *it describes our own situation as well.* We miss the force of the message unless we realize two things: first, when liberation theology describes oppression it is calling us the oppressors; and second, when it tells the peasant that he has been the victim of imperialist aggression, it is saying that white people (probably Americans) are the imperialist aggressors.

As we gird our loins to resist such categorizations, we must pause long enough to realize that at the very least this is the way we *appear* to an increasingly large segment of the human family, and we must be sufficiently humbled by that realization to ask ourselves whether the description may not be closer to the truth than we would be willing to admit simply on the basis of self-scrutiny.

To entertain such a possibility is to be in the first stages of our own experience of conscientization. And, as we have already seen, no one knows where that may lead.

5. To the degree that we do some or all of the above, we will be better equipped to face the basic question, already asked: *can a theology for the oppressed also become a theology for the oppressors?*

Let us begin our response by taking an emphasis in the message for the oppressed and translating the same message for the oppressors.

To the oppressed, liberation theology is saying something like this:

Things need not remain as they are. God takes sides with you and offers you his help in your struggle for the full liberation he wills for all. The social structures that are destroying you must themselves be destroyed. Together you can forge the tools for your own coming emancipation. Your future is increasingly open to the degree that you affirm these things.

If we translate that into a message to the oppressors, liberation theology says, at least initially, something like this:

Things must not remain as they are. God takes sides against you and denies you his help when you deny to others the full liberation he wills for all. The social structures that benefit you are destroying others, and must themselves be destroyed. You cannot forge the tools for your ongoing emancipation by denying similar tools to those who are not yet free. Your future is increasingly closed to the degree that you deny these things.

Why can we not respond more immediately to the message? Surely our greatest difficulty is the insistent affirmation that not only individuals but the entire social structure needs to be reconstituted. To acknowledge that we are individually self-centered and need to become more sensitive to the needs of others is a message we may not like, but it is a message with which we could come to terms: we could give away a little more of our incomes, open our homes to meetings on social causes, devote more time to human relationships. But to acknowledge that our entire social structure is sick at the core is not only a message we may not like, but a message with which we may not, in fact, be able to come to terms: it may challenge the social legitimacy of the kind of work we do to earn our incomes, it may leave us with the nagging question of why we are entitled to such splendid homes when most of the human family lives in substandard dwellings, and it may leave us unsure that the creation of a few splendid human relationships is really a sufficient answer to the not-so-splendid squalor that continues unchallenged in the midst of those relationships.

Such unease will at least be a step toward rethinking the faith by which we presently live, and challenging the adequacy and even the legitimacy of many of the commitments we have previously taken for granted. And as long as the voices issuing that challenge remain insistent enough (as in this day and age they surely will) we may be forced to the point of some crucial decisions about the future direction of our lives.

Whatever those directions may be, we must avoid any tinge of romanticism in working them through. Third World leaders as diverse as Ivan Illich of Mexico and Dom Helder Camara of Brazil urge us, for example, not to go to Latin America to "help people" there, or try to stir up a revolution on somebody else's turf. South Americans have had enough economic and political imperialism from North Americans in the past not to want any cultural or theological imperialism from North Americans in the future. Blacks in the United States would issue a similar reminder that the white person's task is not in the black ghetto but in the white ghetto, working for change within the power structures where whites may conceivably have some leverage.

And that is surely part of the message. Since so much of the human problem today is posed by the irresponsible use of power, and since so much of that power is located within the United States, and since the abuse of that same power works both against oppressed minorities at home and against oppressed majorities abroad, the message to oppressors begins to be pretty clear: work where we are for basic changes in the way we use and abuse our political and economic power, and seek ways in which those who have been denied power can be given a share of it.

There is obviously no neat blueprint for implementing such a widespread mandate, and it is important to realize that there are almost innumerable places to begin, and things to do, that are beyond the possibility of full discussion in the present chapter. But wherever we start, our starting point should involve a new attempt to see ourselves and our world through eyes other than our own, and to move from that new angle of vision to the beginning of acts of identification with the oppressed, putting bodies where words alone were once put. In corporations this may mean not only challenging practices that have a racist tinge, but going on to look for ways to challenge the whole corporate structure that perpetuates injustice. It may mean not only challenging politicians who want to "keep America first" in a world that cannot tolerate one nation having such power, but going on to challenge the political process itself to the degree that it settles for tinkering around the edges instead of working for radical change.

These or similar actions will initially be difficult because they will threaten the structures that have sustained us—corporations, ordinary political loyalties, and so on. It will be difficult too, to let others call the shots and be willing to have the oppressed themselves indicate what things they must do, and what things they are willing to let us do with them.

As this begins to happen, however, we may be able, very slowly, to appropriate for ourselves some of the positive message of liberation theology. We may be able, very slowly, to hear it as a message that not only condemns us but can liberate us as well—from the middle-class hangups that keep us timid, from the frantic need for financial security and social acceptability that enables us to rationalize disengagement, from the hesitancy that prefers the known to the unknown, from the limited perspectives that make it almost impossible to entertain viewpoints other than our own. Our liberation will be of a different sort from that of Brazilian peasants or Harlem blacks, and it will be phony if it is purchased at the cost of keeping them mired in their oppression. But a time must come when our goals and theirs come closer and closer to convergence—liberation *from* structures that are oppressive for any of the human family, liberation *for* a future giving the possibility of full humanness to all and no longer just to a few. And a time must also come when the critique we were previously not entitled to make will be appropriate and necessary, so that not all things are blessed in the name of an uncritical ideology, and so that a healthy distance is maintained between what we actually do and what we describe as God's will.

Such a stance will not be easy to achieve. There will be hostility from those we forsake for a newfound freedom, and suspicion on the part of those we seek to join, who will feel that our conversion is only expedient or temporary or half-hearted. We will learn the hard truth of what Joseph had to learn, in W. H. Auden's "For the Time Being":

> To choose what is difficult all one's days
> As if it were easy, that is faith. . . .

The Abrahamic Venture

It may seem as though we have gone off on a strange tangent in this chapter. Having devoted most of our previous discussion to such things as theology, history, knowing, and doubting, we are suddenly into an almost technical discussion of politics and economics and strategies of radical change. Hasn't the argument gone off the track?

The answer must be an emphatic "no." The whole point of the present chapter is to insist that where faith is at issue, the payoff is whether or not it leads to our being "poured into life," as Martin Buber put it. Liberation theology is simply the most vivid and compelling example for our day of what is at stake. It helps to demonstrate our fundamental thesis that there is an ongoing dialectic between faith and doing, a dialectic that goes like this: Faith leads us to involvement, the involvement helps us refine (and probably redefine) our initial faith, so that that faith can lead us to more significant involvement at a deeper level that helps us refine (and probably redefine) our already re-refined (and probably re-redefined) faith, so that that faith can lead us to more significant involvement at a still deeper level . . . and so on, world without end.

Further insight and deeper commitment will surely come along the way, if the faith is sound, but *they will not be there fully at the start,* and it is this fact that entitles us to describe our situation as participation in the Abrahamic venture.

Abraham, we remember, had it pretty well made in Ur of the Chaldees: he had many flocks, many servants, much wealth—all the comfort and security for which one could ask—and no reason whatever to place it in jeopardy. But there came upon him a compulsion, understood as response to a divine visitation, to risk all that, to place his security in absolute jeopardy and go elsewhere with no guarantees in advance. As one of the New Testament writers reflects on the situation:

> By faith Abraham obeyed when he was called to go out . . . and he went out, not knowing where he was to go. By faith he sojourned . . . as in a foreign land, living in tents with Isaac and Jacob. . . . (Heb. 11:8–9.)

The description is truncated, and in a moment we must fill in the ellipses. But let us notice before doing so that the sparse description is all that Abraham could have been sure of ahead of time. He was called, and he went, "not knowing where he was to go," and when he finally got there it wasn't like home, and he was never really able to settle down. To his friends he must have seemed a fool: he forsook a sure thing and all he got in return was permanent instability.

The author of the account tells us more about Abraham's journey than that, but he tells it from the vantage point of at least two millennia of historical hindsight. We may quote the author's fuller version only if we remember that what is now added in brackets was hidden from Abraham's view and could not have been anticipated or counted upon by him:

> By faith Abraham obeyed when he was called to go out [to a place which he was to receive as an inheritance;] and he went out, not knowing where he was to go. By faith he so-

journed [in the land of promise,] as in a foreign land, living in tents with Isaac and Jacob, [heirs with him of the same promise. For he looked forward to the city which has foundations, whose builder and maker is God.] (Heb. 11:8–10.)

In the expanded version, the place to which Abraham is to go is a place that he is to "receive as an inheritance"; it is a "land of promise," and his sons are "heirs with him of the same promise," even though none of that was assured ahead of time, and the subsequent history of Abraham's descendants even raises questions about whether the optimistic projections may not, even yet, be wishful thinking. Furthermore, as we saw in Chapter Two, Abraham and the other "heroes of faith" mentioned in the Hebrews account are sustained because they look forward "to the city which has foundations [not tents], whose builder and maker is God" (Heb. 11:10). If we recall the difficulties their commitment entailed ("stoned . . . sawn in two"), we can be fairly sure that only some such faith could have sustained them in the face of a subsequent history so devoid of empirical vindication.

There are surely analogies here as we confront our own situation. Faced by demands as challenging as liberation theology, we too are "called to go out" to a new kind of situation, "not knowing where [we are] to go," or exactly what will be asked of us. Our displacement may not be geographical, as was Abraham's, but it will surely be ideological, theological, political, economic, and social. We may be asked to risk all the securities we have accumulated, and to put on the line everything that up to this time has given our lives a sense of stability, order, and even respectability. To dwell where we have always dwelt may be in the new situation to dwell "as in a foreign land," misunderstood or unwanted, while to be less sure of our physical or financial well-being than formerly, may be our modern equivalent of "living in tents."

But along with all that, to take the risk may only be possible for us if we too believe that in this direction lies the fulfillment—not just for us but for all humanity—of "the city which has foundations, whose builder and maker is God."

To take the risk is at least to open a way for the fulfillment of the vision.

But to fail to take the risk is to deny the vision altogether.

FROM DOING ALONE TO DOING TOGETHER

The prescription may seem hopelessly ambitious and demanding. How can we really engage in risk-taking? How can we talk about putting things on the line? Where does the courage come from?

There is a resource available to which we have as yet given little attention, the resource of a community of faith, in which we can sometimes be empowered to do together the things we would scarcely be willing to undertake alone, and we must now look briefly at ways in which community can nurture and strengthen the life of faith.

No Faith Is an Island;
or, John Donne Revised

(faith and community)

> The life of faith is life in the community of faith,
> not only in its communal activities and institu-
> tions but also in the inner life of its mem-
> bers. . . . There is no life of faith, even in mys-
> tical solitude, which is not life in the community
> of faith.
>
> —*Paul Tillich*

John Donne reminded us several centuries ago
that "no man is an island entire of itself," and that consequently we are all involved in one another's destinies. This
is not only eminently true of our physical lives, but just as
true of our believing lives. We do not believe by ourselves,
as individuals in isolation; we believe as part of a community of believers, whether the community is a Benedictine
monastery, a communist cell, a Protestant congregation, a
Jewish minyan, or a Hindu ashram.

To be sure, we must personally appropriate the faith of the
community to which we belong and make it our own, and
in this sense Luther was right in insisting that everyone has
to do his own believing just as everyone has to do his own
dying. But we need to remember also that the faith we per-

sonally appropriate is the faith *of the community*, and this means that even the most internalized, existential act of personal commitment will bind us into a communal relationship of shared belief with others. Even if the faith I appropriate were somehow brand new, never before conceived, the product of no apparent community save my own internal dialogue with myself, if I really believed it to be true I would perforce share it with others and thus, whether I directly willed it or not, a new community would be created around it.

There exist, then, all about us, what Archbishop Helder Camara of Brazil has called "the Abrahamic minorities," because, like Abraham, they are hoping against hope. Appropriate, indeed, that those who make "the Abrahamic venture" should discover that they can be part of Abrahamic minorities as well.

So faith and community are inextricably joined together. *Community can only be created around a faith; faith can only be creative within a community.* It is ironic, but perhaps appropriate, that the last theme of this book turns out to be the presupposition without which the first word of this book could never have been written.

Let us therefore reflect briefly on ways in which the community nurtures and strengthens the life of faith.

First, the community is *the place where the faith of the individual can be tested against the faith of the community.* The community has a long history; better still, it has a memory, which means that it can put its history to use. The individual has a short history that needs frequent checking against the community's longer history. When an individual Marxist offers a new and exciting twist to the dialectic, party members can say, "Wait a minute! That's just what Bakunin thought, and look where it led him. . . ." When an individual Christian, wanting to preserve Jesus' uniqueness, pushes his divinity so hard as to deny his humanity, there is a communal memory to remind him: "That's docetism, the oldest heresy of all. It nearly destroyed the early church and you'd better see where it leads before you use it to destroy the contemporary church as well."

In such situations as these the individual may genuinely feel that Bakunin—or docetism—was right, and thus feel constrained to break with the community if the community cannot be changed. But the decision will at least be an informed one, taken in the light of a wider range of experience and wisdom that the individual alone can possess.

Both the individual and the community, therefore, exemplify the life of faith as the creative appropriation of an open past.

But such a view of community by itself can lead to timidity and rigidity, the community finally being cast in the role of the preserver of orthodoxy, whether the orthodoxy be Marxist or Christian. So the community must also be a garden for heresy, or at least for the testing of new ideas. It must play a second and opposite role as *the place where the faith of the community can be tested against the faith of the individual.* Any community that is truly a community must be able to suffer fools gladly and even embrace the heretics that threaten its peace. Since communities are almost always careful and conservative, they need the leaven of fresh ideas, along with new interpretations of old ideas, and these are contributions that only the most venturesome within their midst are likely to propound. This is how communities stay alive and grow. High medieval Christianity needed a Francis of Assisi, and fortunately recognized the fact. Late medieval Christianity needed a Martin Luther, and unfortunately did not recognize the fact. Marxism always needs fresh prophets to save it from Stalinist aberrations, and it sometimes does (and sometimes does not) recognize the fact. Communities become rigid and frozen without the input of creative and often irrepressible spirits.

A crucial question for the Roman Catholic community to-

day is whether or not it can respond creatively to the challenge of individual voices as diverse as those of Hans Küng
and Daniel Berrigan, and adapt its communal life to the
demands for change that they place upon it. The very choice
of such individuals symbolizes the intricacy of the interrelationship between individual and communal faith. Some
Catholics insist that both men are heretics, to be suffered
within the community only if they mute their voices; others
believe that they represent more authentic versions of the
faith than the various beliefs and practices they are challenging, and that it is the institution rather than the individual that is heretical.

The community contributes to the life of faith in a third
way, by being *the place where the burden of doubt can be
shared.* Faith, we have been insisting, involves risk. Some
risks, shouldered only by the individual, are too overwhelm-
ing and can only be destructive. At such times, the community can be the place for "the bearing of burdens," where
things too heavy to be borne individually can, at least during
crucial moments, be borne corporately. It need not be a sign
of individual weakness, but rather it can be a sign of communal strength, when an individual can say of the forgiveness of sins or the inevitability of the victory of the prole-
tariat, or whatever: "Look, that part of it just doesn't make
sense to me right now. It did once, and I hope it will again,
but for the moment the rest of you will have to do the believing for me." Such individuals can expect that at some
future time they in their turn will be called upon to do the
believing for others during the others' times of darkness or
indecision, for "the bearing of burdens" goes both ways. Such
sharing is not to be interpreted as an exposure of weakness
but as a gift to be treasured.

Fourthly, the community contributes to the life of faith
by being *the place where faith can be celebrated and em-*

bodied. Most faiths are minority faiths, held by only a small portion of the culture in which they are located, and to proclaim them is usually a case of "singing the Lord's song in a strange land" (Psalm 137), whether "the Lord" is the one described by Mark or Marx. But one can sing in a strange land only so long before one begins to doubt the appropriateness of the tune; there must also be times of singing in chorus with those who not only know the tune but who also believe the words to be true.

And the words must not only be celebrated but embodied. If the message of the community is that love is at the heart of things, then the community must be a place where that love is embodied, since it will often be scorned by those outside the community. If the vision of the community calls for production to flow "from each according to his ability, to each according to his need," the community itself must be a place where the vision is a present reality and not just a future hope, or else the vision may die for lack of concrete realization. The community is a place where the faith can be celebrated and embodied, where its members may draw assurance that their faith is a future possibility for all because it is a present reality for a few.

This indeed is the whole meaning of liturgy, to which we alluded in our Introduction. There is no community that does not create liturgies, actions that dramatize its convictions and that help people to participate in the faith they share by acting it out. People who share the same commitments often share the same meals, and the breaking of bread together is a liturgical action, both *expressing* corporateness and *re-creating* it, whether the occasion is a peace march, a family meal, or a eucharist in an upper room or in a cathedral. Communities gather to remember, in the sense of recalling the past, but also to re-member themselves, to be built up again in their various parts (or members) so that they are more significantly whole than they were before.

Finally, the community contributes to the life of faith by being *the place where faith is energized to turn outward*. Communities cannot remain ingrown, concerned only with their own inner life. They too must exemplify faith as the dynamic interrelationship of content and commitment. They must thrust their members out into the "strange land," into the arenas of life not populated by the community. This is only another way of saying that any community—Marxist, Christian, or whatever—is a missionary, i.e., a "sent-forth" community, whatever term for that outward-turning posture may be used. Individuals are often timid about turning outward, and they need the support and the on-the-scene presence of the rest of the community if they are going to share with others the faith they already share among themselves. The community, then, is not only a base to which the individual can return but also a companion on the outward venture.

So, one is called upon to "sing the Lord's song in a strange land," but one is not called upon to sing a solo. A duet can become a trio and finally a chorus. And the size of the chorus is limited only by the willingness of others to join in the song. No one can ever be forced to make music.

But everyone can be invited.

NOTES AND COMMENTS

In an effort to keep the main text from becoming cluttered, I have put all technical apparatus, along with occasional bibliographical suggestions, in this one place. The literature on faith is endless, and only those works are cited below that have had some influence on the development of the argument and can therefore be of use to readers who want to explore certain issues in more detail.

The quotation from W. H. Auden on the epigraph page is from "For the Time Being, A Christmas Oratorio," and is found in *Collected Longer Poems*, by W. H. Auden, copyright 1944 and renewed 1972 by W. H. Auden. This and later quotations from this poem are used by permission of Random House, Inc.

INTRODUCTION

The Decline and Fall of Faith;
or, Clearing Away the Underbrush

Page 12. Hamilton's essay, "Thursday's Child," originally published in *Theology Today*, is available in Thomas J. J. Altizer and William Hamilton, *Radical Theology and the Death of God* (The Bobbs-Merrill Company, Inc., 1966). The quotation is from p. 87.

Page 14. Jürgen Moltmann's major work is *Theology of Hope* (Harper & Row, Publishers, Inc., 1967). A book of essays, *Religion, Revolution and the Future* (Charles Scribner's Sons, 1969), shows the political implications of his theology. Walter H. Capps, *Time Invades the Cathedral* (Fortress Press, 1972), is a helpful interpretative study of Bloch, Moltmann, and Metz.

Page 17. The full text of Dorothy Sayers' catechism is found in *Creed or Chaos?* (London: Methuen & Co., Ltd., 1947). The quotation is from p. 23.

Page 18. Reinhold Niebuhr's comment on faith, hope, and love is from *The Irony of American History* (Charles Scribner's Sons, 1952), p. 63.

Page 19. The schematized arrangements of faith, hope, and love are derived from a discussion of liturgy in my *Frontiers for the Church Today* (Oxford University Press, 1973), pp. 130–133, where I made a promise (not fulfilled) to develop the matter more fully in the present work.

CHAPTER ONE

Definitions Old and New; or, Clarifying Some Ambiguities

Page 21. The Emily Dickinson quotation is from *Complete Poems of Emily Dickinson* (Little, Brown & Company, 1960), p. 185. I am indebted to Ms. Amanda Langston for the reference.

Page 25. Calvin's definition of faith is found in the *Institutes of the Christian Religion*, ed. by John T. McNeill (The Westminster Press, 1960), Vol. I, p. 551 (Book III, Ch. II, para. 7). Book III, Ch. II, is a lengthy development of the implications of the definition. The subsequent quotations from Calvin are found respectively in para. 19 (p. 565) and para. 6 (p. 549; italics added).

Page 31. Moltmann's comment on the church is from *Religion, Revolution and the Future*, p. 6.

Page 32. The statement about Franz Rosenzweig is from Samuel Hugo Bergman, *Faith and Reason: An Introduction to*

Modern Jewish Thought (Schocken Books, Inc., 1963), p. 81 (italics added).

Page 35. Materials from Père Louis Monden, *Faith: Can Man Still Believe?* (Sheed & Ward, Inc., 1970), are drawn from pp. 16 ff.

The etymological comments of Père Olivier Rabut are contained in his *Faith and Doubt* (Sheed & Ward, Inc., 1967).

Page 39. The discussion of faith as trust draws on Joseph Ratzinger, *Faith and the Future* (Franciscan Herald Press, 1971), and the quotations are from pp. 20 and 24 respectively.

In addition to the works cited above, the following are helpful in expanding a definitional approach to faith: D. M. Baillie, *Faith in God* (Edinburgh: T. & T. Clark, 1927), a somewhat older work; Henry Bouillard, *The Logic of the Faith* (Sheed & Ward, Inc., 1967), a variety of essays on the place of faith in the contemporary theological scene; Gerhard Ebeling, *The Nature of Faith* (Muhlenberg Press, 1962), a treatment of fifteen doctrinal areas from the standpoint of faith; Abraham Heschel, *God in Search of Man* (Meridian Books, Inc., 1959), a philosophy of Judaism with special insight into the meaning of faith; Richard R. Niebuhr, *Experiential Religion* (Harper & Row, Publishers, Inc., 1972), an original and creative treatment of a number of themes not fully developed in the present work; Raymond Panikkar, "Faith: A Constitutive Dimension of Man," *Journal of Ecumenical Studies* (Spring 1971), a wide-ranging and important essay; Herbert W. Richardson, *Toward an American Theology* (Harper & Row, Publishers, Inc., 1967), especially Ch. 2 on "Five Kinds of Faith"; Thomas A. Sartory, *A New Interpretation of Faith* (The Newman Press, 1968), a creative Roman Catholic advance; Paul Tillich, *Dynamics of Faith* (Harper & Brothers, 1957), still one of the most useful introductory (and advanced) treatments.

CHAPTER TWO

The Uses of the Past;
or, A Lonely Theological Corrective

Page 41. The initial quotation from Martin Buber is from *Between Man and Man* (The Macmillan Company, 1965), p. 33.

Alvin Toffler's comment in *Future Shock* (Random House, Inc., 1970) is from pp. 373–374 (italics added).

Page 46. The quotation from the Seder service is from Cecil Roth (ed.), *The Haggadah* (London: The Soncino Press, 1959), p. 36.

Page 52. Helmut Gollwitzer's reflection on German guilt comes from his preface to Emmi Bonhoeffer, *Auschwitz Trials* (John Knox Press, 1967), p. 9 (italics added).

Documentation on the American analogues to Auschwitz can be found in Seymour Melman *et al.*, *In the Name of America* (New York: Clergy and Laymen Concerned About Vietnam, 1968), Seymour Hersh, *My Lai 4* (Random House, Inc., Vintage Books, 1970), and many other sources.

Page 53. All the novels and essays of Elie Wiesel are available in paperback from Avon Books (except *The Oath*; Random House, Inc., 1973). Sensitive theological reflection on themes with which Wiesel is dealing can be found in Emil L. Fackenheim, *God's Presence in History* (New York University Press, 1970), especially Ch. 3, "The Commanding Voice of Auschwitz."

Page 55. For the quotation from Elie Wiesel, see *Night* (Avon Books, 1969), p. 44.

Page 56. Viktor Frankl's statement is from *Man's Search for Meaning*, rev. ed. (Beacon Press, 1963), p. 137.

Page 58. W. H. Auden's comment on past, present, and future is from his *The Dyer's Hand* (Random House, Inc., Vintage Books, 1968), p. 430.

Pages 59–62. Sources for the examples drawn from contemporary literature are: Samuel Beckett, *Waiting for Godot* (Grove Press, Inc., 1954); Jean-Paul Sartre, *No Exit and Three Other Plays* (Random House, Inc., Vintage Books, 1946); Simone de Beauvoir, *The Force of Circumstance* (London: George Weidenfeld and Nicholson, Ltd., 1965); Robert J. Lifton, *Revolutionary Immortality* (Random House, Inc., Vintage Books, 1968); Ignazio Silone, *Bread and Wine* (Atheneum Publishers, 1962). There is a further treatment of Pietro Spina, Silone's protagonist, in R. W. B. Lewis, *The Picaresque Saint* (J. B. Lippincott Company, 1961).

Pages 63–64. The quotations here cited from Ratzinger, *Faith and the Future*, are from pp. 30, 32, and 91 respectively.

Materials on the overall themes of faith and history that have been particularly helpful are the following: Hannah Arendt, *Between Past and Future*, rev. and enlarged ed. (The Viking Press, Inc., 1968), on the tension between the two; Herbert Butterfield, *History and Human Relations* (London: William Collins Sons & Co., Ltd., 1951), on making historical judgments; John S. Dunne, *A Search for God in Time and Memory* (The Macmillan Company, 1969), on creative appropriation of the past; Van A. Harvey, *The Historian and the Believer* (The Macmillan Company, 1966), on the tension between the two; Martin E. Marty, *The Search for a Usable Future* (Harper & Row, Publishers, Inc., 1969), which is also the discovery of a usable past; Reinhold Niebuhr, *The Self and the Dramas of History* (Charles Scribner's Sons, 1955), on individual and communal appropriation; Dietrich Ritschl, *Memory and Hope* (The Macmillan Company, 1967), on ways to appropriate past and future; Page Smith, *The Historian and History* (Random House, Inc., Vintage Books, 1966), on criteria of historical evaluation.

CHAPTER THREE

Faith Within the Groves of Academe;
or, The Possibility that Anselm Was Right After All

Page 66. The initial quotation is from John E. Smith, *The Analogy of Experience* (Harper & Row, Publishers, Inc., 1973). This is one of the best available treatments of the theme of "faith seeking understanding."

Page 69. Martin Buber's development of the distinctions outlined in this chapter is found in *Two Types of Faith* (London: Routledge & Kegan Paul, Ltd., 1951). The quotation is from p. 7.

Page 70. Paul Tillich's treatment of faith as "ultimate concern" is dealt with succinctly in *Dynamics of Faith* and is developed in various parts of his *Systematic Theology*, 3 vols. (The University of Chicago Press, 1951–1963). Informal discussion of the matter is contained in Tillich's answers to student questions in D. M. Brown, *Ultimate Concern: Tillich in Dialogue* (Harper & Row, Publishers, Inc., 1965).

Page 72. H. Richard Niebuhr deals with the life of faith in the university in *Radical Monotheism and Western Culture* (Harper & Brothers, 1960). The quotation is from p. 96.

Page 73. The anthology of essays by ex-Communists, *The God That Failed*, ed. by R. W. S. Crossman (Harper & Brothers, 1950), includes contributions from Arthur Koestler, Richard Wright, Louis Fischer, Ignazio Silone, André Gide, and Stephen Spender. The Silone essay is particularly interesting in relation to other references to him in the present work.

Page 75. The statement by Dr. Rieux is found in Albert Camus, *The Plague* (Alfred A. Knopf, Inc., 1950), pp. 196–197.

Page 76. Werner Heisenberg's comment on faith as risk is from his *The Physicist's Conception of Nature* (Harcourt, Brace and Company, Inc., 1958), pp. 65–66.

Page 81. H. Richard Niebuhr's comment about developing scientific knowledge of the world is from his *The Meaning of Revelation* (The Macmillan Company, 1941), p. 173.

Page 82. The comment on the relationship of God to scientific endeavor is from Alfred North Whitehead, *Science and the Modern World* (The Macmillan Company, 1925), pp. 18–19, and a similar theme has often been expressed subsequently by theologians.

Page 83. Martin Luther's hymn "A Mighty Fortress Is Our God" is based on Ps. 46. Its power is increased by the realization that Luther wrote it with a price on his head. The quotations are from stanzas three and four.

Page 84. The first of the two quotations from Dietrich Bonhoeffer is my own translation of a poem he wrote in prison on New Year's Day in 1945, found in *Widerstand und Ergebung*

(Munich: Chr. Kaiser Verlag, 1966), p. 276. The second quotation is from his letter of July 21, 1944, found in *Letters and Papers from Prison*, enlarged ed. (The Macmillan Company, 1972), pp. 369–370.

CHAPTER FOUR

The Struggle for Faith; or, Faith for the Struggle

Page 86. The quotation from Woody Allen is found in "Selections from the Allen Notebooks," printed in that repository of theological wisdom, *The New Yorker*, Nov. 5, 1973, p. 49.

Page 89. Mrs. Callifer's comment is in Graham Greene, *The Potting Shed* (The Viking Press, Inc., 1957), p. 120.

I have not been able to trace the original source of the quotation from Paul Tillich, but it has been used by Union Theological Seminary in connection with the establishment of an endowed chair in his name.

Page 95. Søren Kierkegaard's thirty-two word statement is from his *Philosophical Fragments* (Princeton University Press, 1962), p. 130.

Page 96. The comments of Blaise Pascal on the difficulty of belief are interspersed throughout his *Pensées*.

Page 98. The tension between belief in God and the reality of evil is the most threatening of all areas of Christian belief. The following is a sampling of treatments from a variety of viewpoints: George A. Buttrick, *God, Pain, and Evil* (Abingdon Press, 1966), is a pastoral approach. Langdon Gilkey, *Maker of Heaven and Earth* (Doubleday & Company, Inc., 1959), deals with evil in the context of the doctrine of creation. Roger Hazelton, *God's Way with Man* (Abingdon Press, 1956), and Albert C. Outler, *Who Trusts in God* (Oxford University Press, 1967), both deal with evil in the context of the theme of providence. John H. Hick, *Evil and the God of Love* (Harper & Row, Publishers, Inc., 1968), is the fullest contemporary theological treatment, both historically and systematically. Paul Ricoeur, *The Symbolism of*

Evil (Harper & Row, Publishers, Inc., 1967), is a philosophical approach concentrating particularly on the creation stories. Peter De Vries, *The Blood of the Lamb* (Little, Brown & Company, 1962), is a poignant fictional outcry against a God who allows suffering in his world. J. S. Whale, *The Christian Answer to the Problem of Evil* (London: SCM Press, Ltd., 1936), is a very brief treatment of classical and orthodox Christian approaches to the problem of evil.

Page 105. The brief Auden quotation is from "For the Time Being, A Christmas Oratorio," in *Collected Longer Poems.*

Page 106. The Good Friday statement by Ignazio Silone is found in *And He Did Hide Himself* (London: Jonathan Cape, Ltd., 1946), p. 6.

Page 107. The affirmation by the dying priest is from Georges Bernanos, *Diary of a Country Priest* (Doubleday & Company, Inc., Image Books, 1954), p. 232.

Page 109. The centrality of structure (*Gestalt*) in Bonhoeffer's theology is emphasized in André Dumas, *Dietrich Bonhoeffer: Theologian of Reality* (The Macmillan Company, 1971), especially in Chs. 2, 3, and 8. Bonhoeffer's own central dealings with the matter of structure are found in his early dissertations, *The Communion of Saints* (Harper & Row, Publishers, Inc., 1964), and *Act and Being* (Harper & Brothers, 1962); also in his lectures on Christology, *Christ the Center* (Harper & Row, Publishers, Inc., 1966); and in his posthumously published *Ethics* (The Macmillan Company, 1965). It is the latter work that deals in most detail with deputyship. The Bonhoeffer quotation is from *Ethics*, p. 195.

Page 112. Abraham Heschel deals with the relation of space and time in *The Sabbath* (Meridian Books, 1963), and the quotation is from p. 6. Further reinforcing comments are found on pp. 116–117.

Karl Barth's treatment of creation and covenant is found in *Church Dogmatics*, III/1 (Edinburgh: T. & T. Clark, 1958), the first of four "part-volumes" in Vol. III (The Doctrine of Creation).

CHAPTER FIVE

Faith for the Struggle;
or, The Struggle for Faith

Page 116. The initial quotation by Martin Buber is from *I and Thou*, in the new translation by Walter Kaufmann (Charles Scribner's Sons, 1970), p. 164. The two further quotations from Buber (pages 117 and 118, below) are from the same section, pp. 162 and 163 respectively.

Cardinal Suhard's statement is from his pastoral letter *Priests Among Men* (Fides Press, 1951), p. 50.

Page 118. Arthur Miller's play *Incident at Vichy* is published by Bantam Books, Inc. (1967). The material quoted is found on pp. 85–87. Miller also deals with the theme of guilt in an earlier play, *All My Sons*, available in *Arthur Miller's Collected Plays* (The Viking Press, Inc., 1957).

Page 120. I have dealt with the theme of "faith and doing" in a variety of other works and have not thought it appropriate to recapitulate such material here. Those who wish, however, to see the present discussion in a fuller theological context can refer to my *The Spirit of Protestantism* (Oxford University Press, 1961), Chs. 9, 15, and 16; *The Ecumenical Revolution*, revised and expanded ed. (Doubleday & Company, Inc., 1969), Chs. 19 and 20; *The Pseudonyms of God* (The Westminster Press, 1972), Part III; and *Frontiers for the Church Today* (Oxford University Press, 1973), Chs. 3 to 5 and 7 to 9.

Some of the most useful books on liberation theology are noted in the bibliography of my *Religion and Violence* (The Westminster Press, 1973), pp. 110–112. The fullest treatment is Gustavo Gutiérrez, *A Theology of Liberation* (Orbis Books, 1972). Materials on the shift from development to liberation are cited in the same bibliography, pp. 109–110. The best resource for English readers on contemporary developments on the Latin-American scene is *IDOC International* ("International Documentation on the Contemporary Church"), North American

Edition, New York, N.Y. Orbis Books, Maryknoll, N.Y., has been the pioneer in publishing translations of major works by Third World theologians.

Page 124. The theme of "conscientization" has been developed in the important work by Paulo Freire, *Pedagogy of the Oppressed* (Herder & Herder, Inc., 1972). See also his *Education for Critical Consciousness* (The Seabury Press, Inc., 1973), and his *Cultural Action for Freedom* (London: Penguin Books, Ltd., 1972). A full bibliography of Freire materials is contained in Stanley Grabowski (ed.), *Paulo Freire: A Revolutionary Dilemma for the Adult Educator* (Syracuse University Publications, Program in Continuing Education, 1972), pp. 93–116.

Page 130. The Geneva conference on "Black Theology and Latin American Theology of Liberation" is reported in *Risk* (Geneva: World Council of Churches), Vol. 9, No. 2. This includes the papers of the four speakers, an account of press reaction, and a transcript of some of the important exchanges in the discussion period. The quotations from James Cone are found on pp. 63 and 65.

Page 135. Comments by Third World theologians on the task of those from rich countries can be found in Helder Camara, *Church and Colonialism* (London: Sheed & Ward, Ltd., 1969), especially Ch. 10, and, more sharply, in Ivan Illich, *The Church, Change and Development* (Herder & Herder, Inc., 1970), especially pp. 42–53. The fullest treatments of "black theology" are in James H. Cone, *Black Theology and Black Power* (The Seabury Press, Inc., 1969); *A Black Theology of Liberation* (J. B. Lippincott Company, 1970); and *The Spirituals and the Blues* (The Seabury Press, Inc., 1972). J. Deotis Roberts, *Liberation and Reconciliation: A Black Theology* (The Westminster Press, 1971), is a somewhat different approach. Gayraud S. Wilmore, *Black Religion and Black Radicalism* (Doubleday & Company, Inc., Anchor Books, 1973), is a full and very useful historical treatment.

Page 137. We have quoted these lines on the epigraph page of this book. From Auden, "For the Time Being, A Christmas Oratorio," in *Collected Longer Poems*.

EPILOGUE

*No Faith Is an Island;
or, John Donne Revised*

A number of the themes suggested in the Epilogue have been developed in fuller detail in my *Frontiers for the Church Today*, which also contains an annotated bibliography (pp. 136–143).

Page 141. The Tillich quotation is from *Dynamics of Faith*, p. 118.